10 June 2008, Latrun

Dear Wilma,

"...and maketh us wiser than the fowls of heaven…"(Job 35,11)

I Hope to fly you with the glider & birds!

I have the pleasure and honor of presenting you with the book "Flying with the Birds" - the story of the joint research project with the Israel Air Force that led to peaceful coexistence between steel winged "birds" and their feathered companions in the skies.

Chapter 7 ('taking off Into the Third Millennium") has been added to the Hebrew edition and presents the activity of the International Center for the Study of Bird Migration, that is now being built at Latrun, taking off into new horizons…

warmest Regards
and friendship,

Yossi Leshem

Tel Aviv University
אוניברסיטת תל אביב

המרכז הבינלאומי לחקר
נדידת הציפורים בלטרון
The International Center
for the Study of Bird
Migration, Latrun

The Society for the Protection of Nature in Israel

המרכז הבינלאומי לחקר נדידת הציפורים בלטרון
THE INTERNATIONAL CENTER FOR THE STUDY OF BIRD MIGRATION, LATRUN

Dr. Yossi Leshem
Director
e-mail: yleshem@post.tau.ac.il
mobile: **+972-52-3257722**
our website: www.birds.org.il אתרנו באינטרנט:

Office:
Telefax: 972-3-6406010
Tel: 972-3-6407963
Tel Aviv University
George S. Wise Faculty of Life
Sciences, Department of Zoology,
Ramat Aviv, Tel Aviv 69978, Israel

Home:
Telefax: 972-2-9932629
Tel: 972-2-9932308

Home Address:
Har Gilo, Doar Na Zfon
Yehuda 90907 Israel

The Society for the Protection of Nature in Israel

Flying with
the Birds

High Flight

Oh, I have slipped the surly bonds of earth,
And danced the skies on laughter-silvered wings;
Sunward I've climbed and joined the tumbling mirth
Of sun-split clouds-and done a hundred things
You have not dreamed of-wheeled and soared and swung
High in the sunlit silence. Hov'ring there,
I've chased the shouting wind along and flung
My eager craft through footless halls of air.
Up, up the long delirious, burning blue
I've topped the wind-swept heights with easy grace,
Where never lark, or even eagle, flew;
And, while with silent, lifting mind I've trod
The high untrespassed sanctity of space,
Put out my hand, and touched the face of God.

John Gillespie Magee, Jr.

Yossi Leshem • Ofer Bahat

Flying with the Birds

Tel-Aviv University

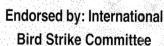
Endorsed by: International Bird Strike Committee

Ministry of Science

Yedioth Ahronoth Chemed Books

The Society for the Protection of Nature in Israel

The Israel Air Force

FLYING WITH THE BIRDS
Yossi Leshem • Ofer Bahat

Translation: **Esther Lachman**

Design and Production: **Studio Igal Rosenthal**

Line Drawings: **James P. Smith**

Color sketches and maps: **Tuvia Kurtz**

Graphic performance: **Bela Genis**

Production Manager: **Dani Barzilay**

Print: **Kal Press**

Aircraft Photographs: **By courtesy of the IAF magazine**

Cover Photos: **Duby Tal - Albatross & Paul Doherty**
F-16D fighter planes and Honey Buzzards flying over the Galilee

Printed in Israel 1999

362-1555

ISBN: 965-448-518-4

Table of Contents

Introduction

The President - Mr. Ezer Weizman 11

The Commander of the Israel Air Force - Maj. Gen. Eitan Ben-Eliahu 13

Preface 15

Chapter One: Migration - the "Eighth Wonder"

A. Migration in the Animal World 21

B. Bird Migration - Scope and Causes 43

C. How Bird Flight Principles are Applied in Migration 53

D. How Birds Find Their Way on Migration 70

E. Timing of Migration, Fat Storage and "Refueling" 77

Chapter Two: Israel - A Crossroads between Three Continents

A. Israel's Unique Position on the World Migration Map 85

B. Soaring Birds Migrating over Israel 87

C. Migrating Birds - Chances of Survival 90

Chapter Three: Aircraft and Birds - Conflict or Coexistence?

A. The Vast Damages Suffered by the Israel Air Force from Migrating Birds ... 109

B. From the Fighter Pilots' Mouths - a Series of Severe Collisions with Birds ... 111

C. The Conflict Between Birds and Aircraft in other Parts of the World 125

Chapter Four: The Study of Bird Migration in Israel

A. The History of Bird Migration Study 133

B. Bird Ringing 134

C. Ground-based Observers 143

D. Light Aircraft 144

E. The Motorized Glider 144

F. Unmanned Aircraft (Drone) 147

G. Radar 148

H. Combined Methods 151

Chapter Five: Study Results

A. Migration Routes, Altitudes and Times 159

B. Migration Axis Daily Fluctuations 161

C. Migration Axis Seasonal and Annual Fluctuations 162

D. Flight Speed and Other Characteristics 166

E. Daily and Seasonal Progress Rate 167

F. Biological Factors and their Effect on Migrating Birds 170

G. Weather Effects on Soaring Bird Migration 179

H. The Bird Plagued Zone (BPZ) Map 187

I. The Significant Reduction of Bird-Aircraft Collisions 188

J. The Effect of Migration on Birdwatching in Israel 193

Chapter Six: How to Watch Migrating Birds in Israel

A. Observation Methods 197

B. Recommended Birdwatching Sites 198

C. Migration Dates 204

Chapter Seven: Taking Off Into the Third Millennium

A. The Bird Migration Center at Latrun, Israel -
Beating Swords Into Ploughshares 213

B. Satellites Research 221

C. Establishment of a Radar Network in the Middle East 236

D. The Center at Latrun - Migration, a First Rate Educational Tool 239

E. Migrating Birds Play a Leading Role in the Middle East Peace Process 243

F. The Development of Regional Ecotourism and Birdwatching 250

G. Information and Public Activity 254

INTRODUCTION

The President

In the summer of 1948, Israel waged its War of Independence, its Air Force was still in infancy, and I had the honor of taking part in transferring the first real fighter aircraft to our country following 2000 years of exile - the "Messerschmitt".

Squadron 101, in which I flew, had many successes on all fronts in the bitter fight to keep the enemy at bay. One morning I was sent to attack Jordanian tanks in the center of the country. While diving and shooting at the targets in the midst of dense anti-aircraft fire the front window of my aircraft shattered and several holes appeared in its wings.

I landed, and was met by Sergeant-major Yehuda Pilpel, one of the few mechanics in the Air Force at that time. I told him dramatically: "I seem to have been hit", and was silent. Pilpel examined the plane and pulled out a bird that had collided with the window and smashed it... For many years after Pilpel would joke at my expense about that "mischievous" bird.

The "battle" between birds and fighter aircraft has plagued the Israel Air Force since its establishment. The problem is especially serious in a small country such as Israel, with its limited air space. It has been our luck to be situated so uniquely, at the junction of three continents, and thus blessed with the densest bird migration in the world.

As a pilot I can but not wonder at this singular natural phenomenon, with migrating birds arriving year after year with precise timing, navigating accurately from distances greater than 10,000 kilometers. Their unmatched command of air currents and their ability to soar and glide for 10-11 continuous hours have always fired my imagination.

When I was Minister of Science and Technology, I was personally involved in financing the research done by Yossi Leshem. I am well acquainted with the remarkable results of this joint project undertaken by the Israel Air Force and the Society for the Protection of Nature in Israel. Thanks to it, the number of collisions between fighter aircraft and migrating birds has been dramatically reduced, and the project has become a model for western air forces.

These days - when the bells of peace sound in our land - migrating birds, which know no political boundaries, have greater significance than ever before. I am certain that the story of this study, as told here, will serve as a model for the Arab countries neighboring us, both for peaceful coexistence of birds and aircraft and for nations in the area.

Ezer Weizman
President of Israel

The Commander of the Israel Air Force

The State of Israel lies between the Syrian-African Rift to the east and the Mediterranean Sea to the west, a sliver of land directly on the route of birds migrating between Europe and Africa.

There is a significant amount of air traffic over Israel - both from domestic airlines as well due to intensive training by the Israel Air Force (IAF). In order for both metal and living birds to coexist in harmony, the available airspace must be divided to avoid dangerous and deadly accidents.

For years many flights were conducted over Israel without fully understanding the flight patterns of the birds that shared these skies. Dr. Yossi Leshem of the Society for the Protection of Nature in Israel and Tel Aviv University conducted a study in conjunction with the IAF, during which we learned about the wonderful world of the birds that share our airspace.

Since the study was completed the IAF has changed its flights to avoid contact between birds and aircraft - enabling us to conduct necessary training while minimizing airborne collisions.

Over the past few years the implementation of the study's results has proven itself. The study should serve as a good example to other air forces to demonstrate how man and birds can share the skies.

Maj. Gen. Eitan Ben-Eliahu
Commander, Israel Air Force

Does the hawk fly by your wisdom, and stretch her wings toward the south? (Job 39:26)

Preface

Anyone who has ever seen an eagle soaring majestically one moment and suddenly stooping to its prey the next, at over 200 kilometers an hour, knows that Israel would not be the same place without migrating birds. Anyone who has ever watched a giant flock of thousands of storks circling in a thermal realizes that birds are an integral part of our landscape.

Our forefathers in ancient times were already impressed by the power of birds of prey, their strong, curved beaks, their immense wingspread and their long, sharp talons. The eagle and the vulture were revered in ancient Egypt, Greece and Rome and sacred in many other ancient cultures. Only noblemen were permitted to raise and train raptors for hunting.

No wonder so many fighter planes are called after birds of prey such as the hawk, the eagle and the falcon, just as it is only natural that the stork symbolizes spring, the home and hearth and the major "baby provider" the world over.

Israel's unique location, at the junction of three continents, has always been a powerful focus for international political strife. On the other hand this also makes the country a "bottleneck" and crossroads for bird migration unequalled by almost any other area in the world. Studies from the last decade show that about 500 million migrating birds (!) fly over Israel's limited air space twice yearly, transforming Israel into a virtual Mecca for bird lovers from the world over, who come to watch and enjoy this fantastic natural phenomenon.

This massive migration has created a serious flight safety problem for Israel Air Force planes and a very real threat to pilot lives. This book describes the fascinating story of the study done by Yossi Leshem for his Ph.D. degree, with the cooperation of the Israel Air Force (IAF), the Society for the Protection of Nature in Israel (SPNI), Tel Aviv University and others. By using a combination of innovative thinking and methods, that include light aircraft, motorized gliders, drones, radar and an extensive ground observer network we succeeded in solving the problem of bird-aircraft collisions almost completely within a few short years. The IAF could now continue its intensive maneuvers in Israel's narrow airspace while reducing accidents by 76%! The implementation of the study's recommendations has saved pilot lives as well as expensive equipment, while protecting the millions of migrating birds that converge into our skies for seven months out of every year.

More than 300 people were involved in gathering the data for Yossi Leshem's thesis, participating in migration surveys, watching radar screens, flying the motorized glider and operating the extensive research complex. The names of all these would fill a book, and so we would like to express our heartfelt gratitude to all those who helped and took part in the study. Many did this on a completely volunteer basis, working jointly as a team striving to achieve a common goal - the success of the project.

This study would never have succeeded without the IAF, the principal patron and full time partner in financing the study, both during its development and later its successful implementation within the air force. We would like to express here our gratitude to the many IAF officers who took an active part in advancing the research, from IAF commanders Maj. Gen. (res.) Amos Lapidot, who began the project, his successor Maj. Gen. (res.) Avihu Bin-Nun, during whose time most of the study was done, and his successor Maj. Gen. (res.) Herzl Bodinger and to Eitan Ben-Eliahu

Page 14:
A Pelican taking-off from the water.
(Photo: Eyal Bartov)

15

Front Plate:
A Phantom fighter and an
Imperial Eagle.
(Drawing: James P. Smith)

Page 2:
An F-15 fighter plane flying through
the clouds.
(Photo courtesy of the Israel Air Force)

Page 3:
White Storks preparing to fly off
on migration.
(Photo: Yig'al Livneh)

Page 4:
White Stork flying in the sunset.
(Photo: Pierre Perin)

Page 5:
The motorized glider flying with storks.
(Drawing: James P. Smith)

Page 6:
Lesser Spotted Eagles on migration.
(Drawing: James P. Smith)

Pages 8-9:
F-16 fighter planes flying over Massada.
(Photo: Duby Tal, Albatross Inc.)

Page 10:
An adult Bearded Vulture in flight.
(Photo: N. Denis, Panda Photo)

Page 12:
An F-15i fighter plane of the
Israel Air-Force over the Dead-sea.
(Photo: Duby Tal, Albatross Inc.)

the present commander of the IAF. We would also like to thank the Flight Safety Unit officers and the radar units whose cooperation made the results of our study an integral part of IAF procedures, and the Intelligence officers and crew who operated the Drones, with whom we discovered and developed new research methods for the first time ever.

Prof. Yoram Yom-Tov, as academic supervisor, was invaluable throughout the study with his scientific insight, tireless supervising and door always open and welcoming. Prof. Heinrich Mendelssohn, Prof. Amotz Zahavi and Prof. Lev Fishelson were a constant source of encouragement and new ideas. Thanks also to Dr. Ian Newton and Prof. Uriel Safriel for our productive talks and discussions.

Israel is blessed with talented and devoted birdwatchers many of whom helped and participated in this study: Ehud Dovrat, a pioneer in the field, Dan Alon, the director of the Israel Ornithology Center, Hadoram Shirihai, Yaron Bazar, Ariel Sobol, Kobi Merom are only a few who helped all along the way. Many others, more than these few lines can contain, participated and swept hundreds of volunteers in their wake, from Israel and abroad, with their enthusiasm to follow migration and become part of the now regular ground observer team spread across the country during migration.

The devoted motorized glider pilots, Eli Peretz - director of the "Ayit" company, Michael Pinkus, Adi Grinberg, Shahar Goldberg, Rena Levinson, Rafi Luski and others spent hundreds of flight ours with us gliding and soaring with the migrating birds, a thrilling experience second to none.

We would also like to thank the Ministry of Science and Technology that helped fund the study, particularly the former ministers, the honorable President Ezer Weizman and Prof. Yuval Ne'eman. Dr. Miriam Waldman, Avi Anati and Frida Hasofer all helped and encouraged us expressing constant interest in our progress and results and the Ecological Fund for its part in financing the study.

We extend our thanks to the Israel Airport Authority that placed a radar console at our disposal regularly at the Ben-Gurion International Airport, despite the already heavy workload; to the control tower staff for their unfailing patience; to Pini Magor and Asher Friedman who coordinated the soldiers manning the radar and to Ilana Agat who was of great help with radar work in the early stages of the project.

The migration surveys would not have succeeded without the warm hospitality of the kibbutzim that provided lodging for the many volunteers who participated in the surveys: Tze'elim, Masha'abe Sade, Einat, Sede Boqer, Yagur, G'vat, Genigar, Mizra, Dovrat, En Harod, Tel Yosef, Geva, Shluhot, Mesilot, Gesher, Ma'oz Hayim and Kfar Ruppin. We also thank meteorologists Richard Abramsky and Dr. Noah Wolfson, directors of the Meteo-Tech Corporation, who coordinated the compilation and analysis of the data and the statistical and meteorological analysis with the utmost proficiency in a warm, friendly atmosphere; Nurit Hadas for her competent computer work and the Israel Meteorological Service for gathering the data and permitting us to use them. Hanoch Livneh, the merchandising manager and the Mapping Technologies Company generously provided three-dimensional mapping of the motorized glider flights and Albert Ender (MTL) for his expert work in preparing the maps. The Society for the Protection of Nature in Israel financed a major part of the project. Its many workers expressed constant interest in the study and helped develop it in

16

An F-16 fighter plane in a flock of Cranes.
(Drawing: James P. Smith)

a variety of ways. Thanks also to Miri Shmida and Vered Idelman for preparing the maps; to the dedicated staff of the SPNI Israel Raptor Information Center and Israel Ornithology Center, particularly Haim Alfiya, Yotam Regev, Shlomit Grinblum, Adiv Gal, Judy Shamoun and the many others who often worked late into the night turning from hawks into owls...

We would also like to express our warmest thanks to Maj. Gen. (ret.) Musa Peled, Chairman of the Armored Corps Association and to Brigadier General (ret.) Menashe Inbar and his predecessor Aryeh Keren for their vision and goodwill in agreeing to incorporate the International Center for the Study of Bird Migration into the Armored Corps Memorial Site at Latrun.

This book is a translation of the Hebrew version that was published in 1994, and later reprinted in August 1996. The book won the General Yitzhak Sade Prize for Military Writing, presented in the presence of the late Israeli Prime Minister Mr. Yitzhak Rabin, the Minister of Health Mr. Ephraim Sneh, the Minister of Agriculture Mr. Ya'akov Tsur and the IAF Commander Maj. Gen. Eitan Ben Eliahu. This was the first time ever a nature book won this prestigious prize.

We would like to thank Dudi Eichenwald and Dani Barzilai from the publishers who helped produce the English edition of this book, and spared no work to obtain a result as near perfect as possible. Iigal Rosenthal, the designer, worked skillfully and tirelessly, day and night on the graphic design of the book. Thanks to James P. Smith for his line drawings and to Tuvia Kurtz for the excellent color illustrations and maps; to the photographers who provided some of their best work and to the IAF magazine staff that placed aircraft photos at our disposal.

We would like to express our appreciation to Dr. Dani Simon from the Tel Aviv University Zoology Department, the scientific referee of this book, who gave unstintingly from his time and extensive knowledge to see that not even the smallest mistake remained uncorrected. Thanks to Esther Lachman for translating the text into English combining her biological knowledge and understanding of the English language.

And last but never least to Yossi's devoted wife Rivka and to his five children who usually saw him only in flight, for their patience, encouragement and constant support, without which he would not have gotten off the ground!

Yossi Leshem and Ofer Bahat

Spring Migration, 1999

Page 18:
Steppe Eagles stopping to roost in the Negev.
(Drawing: James P. Smith)

17

Chapter 1

Migration -
the "Eighth Wonder"

שְׁלֹשָׁה הֵמָּה נִפְלְאוּ מִמֶּנִּי וְאַרְבָּעָה לֹא יְדַעְתִּים:

דֶּרֶךְ הַנֶּשֶׁר בַּשָּׁמַיִם דֶּרֶךְ נָחָשׁ עֲלֵי צוּר

דֶּרֶךְ-אֳנִיָּה בְלֶב-יָם וְדֶרֶךְ גֶּבֶר בְּעַלְמָה

(משלי ל', יח-יט)

"There are three things which are too wonderful for me,
Indeed, four which I know not:
The way of a vulture in the sky;
The way of a serpent on a rock;
The way of a ship in the midst of the sea;"
And the way of a man with a young woman.
(Proverbs, 30:18-19)

A. Migration in the Animal World

Bird migration is only one facet of a remarkable natural phenomenon in the animal world that has probably existed since the beginning of time. Migration is the passage from one place to another, for the purpose of reproducing, finding food or escaping difficult climatic conditions that prevent survival. It is usually characterized by regular cycles and movements to and from specific areas. The journeys of birds have attracted interest since days bygone. In the book of Jeremiah we find the verse: "Yea, the stork in the heaven knoweth her appointed times, and the turtledove and the swift and the crane observe the time of their coming" (Jeremiah 8:7). People in ancient times were also well aware of raptor migration. Job, for example, knew their movements well: "Doth the hawk soar by thy wisdom, and stretch her wings toward the south?" (Job, 39:26). The prophet Hosea mentions bird migration as well: "They shall come trembling as a bird out of Egypt, and as a dove out of the land of Assyria" (Hosea, 11:11).

Migration is a motif interwoven widely in the culture of the ancient world. In the 8th century BC, Homer, in the Iliad. compares the Trojan army to cranes escaping from the oncoming winter. Four hundred years later, Anacreon, the Greek poet, described the return of the swallows, and how they spend the winter on the banks of the Nile. Aristotle, the famous Greek scientist and philosopher (384-322 BC), was the greatest animal researcher in the ancient world. In his book on the history of the animal world (Historia Animalium) he devotes an entire chapter to the subject of migration. In it he describes how certain animals do not migrate at all, while others migrate south in the autumn to evade the cold in the north, returning in spring to escape the heat in the south. He claims that all animals grow fatter before leaving on migration. The cranes, according to Aristotle, migrate from Scythia (north of the Black Sea), to southern Egypt, at the sources of the Nile. Pelicans migrate from Strymon in northeast Greece, to the Danube, where they nest. He also describes how they migrate in flocks, with the lead bird waiting for those behind, since when crossing mountains the birds in the rear lose eye contact with the ones ahead. Aristotle's knowledge was not always accurate, and sometimes he erred in its interpretation. One prominent example is his claim that birds that fear the dangers of migration spend the winter sleeping in crevices, after having shed all their feathers. Among those he includes the Swallow, the Kite, the Stork, the Thrush and the Dove. Another mistaken idea of his is that some birds depart and then return as a different species. The Redstart, according to Aristotle, vanishes when autumn comes, reappearing as a Robin. Despite the basic errors in his conceptions they were widely accepted by scientists for the following 2000 years. Oleus Magnus, the archbishop of Uppsala, Sweden, expressed similar ideas in his works, stating that swallows that disappeared in autumn, hibernated under water! The archbishop claimed that fishermen who brought the swallows up in their nets provided this information. Other unfounded ideas about migration included the belief that certain birds grow from trees, while others come forth from shells. These statements were based on the departure of migrating birds to unknown parts for long periods of time and prevailed, in various forms, until the 19th century.

King Friedrich II of Germany (1194-1250), was an exception to this rule, having a remarkable knowledge and understanding of migration. The king practiced falconry and was very interested in, and closely acquainted with the animal world. In his book Arte Venadicum Avibus (The Art of Hunting with Birds), he wrote that birds migrate

A flock of Pelicans migrating over the Hula Valley .
(Photo: Yossi Leshem)

A drawing from the book by Oleus Magnus, 1555, showing fishermen pulling swallows from the water.

Page 20:
American Monarch Butterflies wintering in Mexico.
(Photo: Frans Lanting, Bruce Coleman Limited)

in autumn from cold to warm areas. Not all of them migrate great distances, some merely descend from mountainous areas to lowlands and return to the peaks in spring. He also described the manner in which many birds gather in large groups before migration, sometimes delaying their departure when the weather is good and food abundant. King Friedrich depicted the typical V-formation flight of geese and cranes, claiming that the lead bird invests greater effort in flight and is therefore eventually replaced by another bird.

Orderly and methodical research on migration began only in the 19th century. In its early stages scientists concentrated mainly on birds, whose migration was known best. In time they studied other migrating organisms as well, and distinguished between several different types of migration:

Seasonal back and forth migration - this is the best known type of migration and is typical of many birds. Individuals migrate from breeding grounds to winter quarters, where they can find sufficient food. This type of migration usually occurs back and forth each year. The number of migration voyages is equal to the number of years in an animal's life. This type of migration is also found in certain whales and large ungulates such as the Gnu in East Africa, as well as in humans. Nomadic tribes whose economy is based on grazing, wander with their herds to areas where food is seasonally plentiful, returning at a later date to their point of origin.

Migration by different generations - this type of migration is found in Salmon, who swim upstream to lay their eggs. The Salmon swim upriver to the site where they hatched after having spent a lifetime in the open sea. They spawn and then die, while their offspring swim downstream to the sea.

Emigration - in this type of migration animals go from one site to another never returning to the original site. It is encountered in various plants and animals, and of course, in man.

A migrating Crane.
(Photo: Ofer Bahat)

Although we tend to consider plants as fixed organisms that do not move from place to place, they can actually disperse to great distances, migrating passively over large parts of the globe. One example of the amazing ability of plants to spread can be found in the following case recorded in England in the mid-seventies. A Japanese alga, Saragassum muticum, was discovered on the southern shores of England. The algae spread rapidly along the British coast, until authorities were forced to take emergency measures to prevent it overcoming the local coastal flora. The algae were destroyed wherever found, and fishermen or anyone finding the algae, were requested to eliminate any concentrations they detected. This same species can be found in dense concentrations along the northwestern coast of France and the Belgian coast. Algae and many other non-flowering plants disperse and spread via water currents. Flowering plant seeds can also be found at times in water currents. These are usually coastal plants whose seeds, encapsulated in a membranous envelope which protects them from the salinity of the sea, are disseminated by water currents.

Wind is one of the major agents of seed dispersal in plants. This is especially true for plants with spores or minuscule seeds whose minute weight allows the wind to transport them over great distances. In a study conducted in the Caribbean Islands, researchers found seeds whose mineral content showed them to have originated in the Sahara Desert! In another study, plants and spores were gathered by aircraft, and some of the samples were collected at an altitude of 5000 meters!

Various species of algae, fungi, moss and ferns produce spores so small and light that they are carried by wind over the entire globe. A single fungus produces up to billions of spores, in order to increase its chances of multiplying and spreading.

Flowering plants produce large seeds that are not easily transported by wind. Many species however, have seeds whose aerodynamic structure enables the wind to convey them distances up to hundreds of meters. Among these are seeds whose structure resembles propeller blades that rotate in wind currents, scattering to great distances. This dispersal method is characteristic of various arboreal species such as Pine, Maple and Ash.

Many plants "migrate" with the assistance of animals, usually mammals or birds, but sometimes reptiles as well. Giant sea turtles that migrate great distances over the oceans, play a unique role in seed dispersal. They feed on fruit on one island, later excreting the seeds on another, at times thousands of kilometers away. During this

Seed dispersal in the wind.
(Photo: Kim Taylor, Bruce Coleman Limited)

Pages 24-25:
A small portion of the American Monarch Butterflies wintering in Mexico.
(Photo: R. Austing, FLPA)

Page 27:
American Monarch Butterflies wintering in Mexico.
(Photo: Frans Lanting, Bruce Coleman Limited)

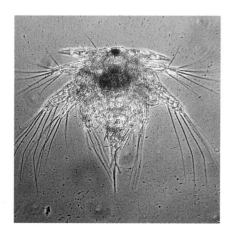

Barnacle larvae migrating.
(Photo: Dr. Frieder Sauer,
Bruce Coleman Limited)

process the seed coat is digested thus facilitating germination. Frugivorous birds and mammals excrete their seeds by a similar process, and so contribute to seed dissemination. Some seeds adhere to the woolly coats of mammals and are carried by them, until they fall off and germinate in new sites. Seeds caught in bird feathers disperse in a similar manner.

Animals, from the most primitive on to man, show migrating ability in all stages of their development. Marine invertebrates migrate largely passively. In many sessile species, migration occurs during some stage of their life cycle. This stage, which can last several weeks or months, allows sessile animals to colonize new sites and compete for new food sources. One such instance is the Goose Barnacle, whose minute larvae are transported long distances by water currents, until a suitable site for colonization, such as a rock near the beach or a piece of wood floating in the sea, is located. At this point the larvae lose their motility and attain adult form. Adults feed by thrusting out and withdrawing their cirri, gathering food particles from the water into the buccal cavity.

The Common Acorn Barnacle has a similar life cycle. Its adult stage is spent on coastal rocks, and it can release more than 10,000 larvae yearly into the sea. Less than one percent of these will reach maturity, the rest succumbing to predation or lack of food.

Studies carried out in the Atlantic Ocean showed that identical sea anemone, mollusk and worm species are found on both sides of the ocean. Samples of larvae collected across the ocean revealed that migration took place in both directions. Larvae released on the western side of the Atlantic, on the North American coast, drifted with the Gulf Stream east to the coast of Europe. Larvae released on the African coast, drifted west with Equatorial currents. Scientists estimate that it takes larvae between 150-300 days to cross the Atlantic in one direction.

The larvae of one Decapoda (Crustacea) species effect an incredible migration. They start out as minute larvae carried on water currents, reaching the adult stage only after 7-9 months, at which time they are 80 centimeters long. A concentration of larvae on the western coast of Australia was marked and tracked by satellite. Some of the larvae were carried west by currents, and during 9 months of migration crossed the Indian Ocean, from east to west, covering a distance of about 6000 kilometers to the eastern coast of Africa.

Among terrestrial invertebrates, the longest-distance migrants are insects. The migration of the American Monarch Butterfly is unique. As autumn approaches, Monarch Butterflies begin their migration south. Migration times and routes are so regular, that there are people along the way who receive them festively year after year. American Monarch Butterflies marked with minute wing tags in the northern United States and Canada, were later located between Texas and the Gulf of Mexico,

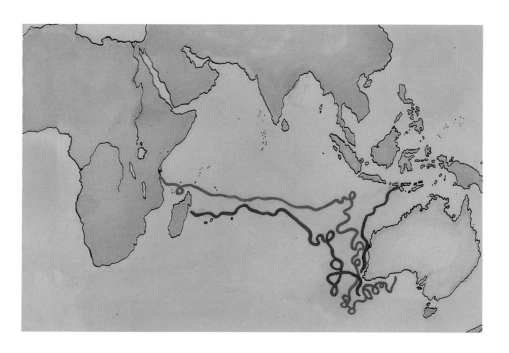

Larvae of a Decapoda (Crustacea) species migration route from Australia to East Africa and Southeast Asia.
(Drawing: Tuvia Kurtz)

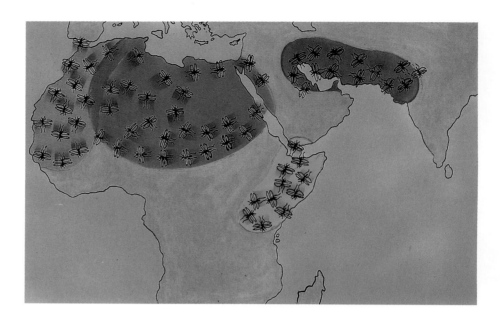

Locust migration map.
(Drawing: Tuvia Kurtz)

2000 to 3000 kilometers from their point of origin. The butterflies overwinter in these areas, some of them clustering in roosts on trees in dense colonies of hundreds and thousands or more. Many of the Monarch Butterflies wintering in the southern United States and Mexico reproduce during the winter, and the adults die several weeks later. Their offspring fly north along the same route used by their parents, with no guidance or help in finding the way.

One of the most conspicuous migrations in insects, is the locust migration. Locust is a general name given to several herbivorous grasshoppers that live either solitarily or in swarms. The change in lifestyle is determined mainly by one factor - the amount of food available. When food is plentiful the solitary locusts breed rapidly and their numbers increase accordingly. As conditions become more crowded, they form swarms, and undergo morphological changes. *Schistocerca gregaria*, a common species from tropical Africa, north to northern Africa, the Middle East and the Arabian peninsula, as well as between Iraq and India, is green when solitary and brown to yellow when in swarms. Females in swarms lay double or more the number of eggs than solitary females. *Schistocerca gregaria* migrates in swarms of tens of millions and sometimes over 100 million individuals, spreading over areas more than 1000 square kilometers! The swarms look like clouds of smoke from afar and as they approach they cover the sky, hiding the sun and darkening the area below. Swarms of locusts have been observed flying with the aid of air currents up to altitudes of 4000 meters. *Schistocerca* migration follows changing rain patterns and their movements may be circular or in a straight line, back and forth. Swarms of locusts sometimes fly hundreds or thousands of kilometers to areas where rain has fallen and food is plentiful. There is locust migration from East Africa (Kenya and Tanzania) north to the Arabian Peninsula and back again. Other populations migrate circularly around the Sahara and the Sahel steppe region south of the Sahara. Swarms from this migration also reach the Middle East and in the past have caused serious damage in Israel. Another locust migration route lies between Iraq and India. When a swarm of locusts lands to feed it destroys any and all vegetation in its way, including the bark of trees, leaving almost nothing. An individual locust consumes an amount equivalent to its body weight daily. Due to the tremendous damage caused by these swarms the locust has been put under international supervision, with steps taken to destroy swarms in order to prevent damage to vegetation and crops. On the other hand, locusts are an important food source for migrating and wintering birds in Africa (such as storks), and eliminating them is detrimental to the birds feeding on them.

Fish belong to another class of long-distance migrants in the animal world, and salmon are among the most conspicuous. Two species of salmon, the European Salmon and the Pacific Salmon, migrate throughout their ranges. Salmons swim upstream, against the current, and even up waterfalls several meters high. They do so in order to reach river sources after having spent their entire life in the open seas. At the end of this journey they lay their eggs, dying a short while after spawning,

28

Locusts consume all vegetation along their migration route.
(Photo: Jane Burton, Bruce Coleman Limited)

The Locust plague that hit Israel in 1915.
(Courtesy of Ariel Publishing House)

while their offspring swim downstream to the sea. Research has shown that every salmon species, and each population, has a different migration range, according to its breeding sites and the sites it inhabits in the open seas. The Pink Salmon is the smallest salmon species in the northern Pacific Ocean. It migrates a maximal distance of about 4000 kilometers to its breeding sites. About 90% of the fish that survive navigate accurately back to their original hatching site. The secret of this navigation apparently lies in their sense of smell and their ability to remember and identify characteristic smells along their way back to their hatching site.

To the best of our knowledge, most reptiles migrate only very short distances, if at all. The exception to this rule are marine turtles. The females dig holes in the sand with their legs and lay eggs in them. The baby turtles, guided by an innate instinct, make their way to the sea immediately after hatching. Young marine turtles roam the seas until they reach maturity, at approximately 12 years of age. Only a few seem to survive, but very little is known about this stage of their life. There is however, information on the adult migration of several marine turtle species, such as the Green Turtle. The Green Turtle is found in all tropical oceans, where temperature does not

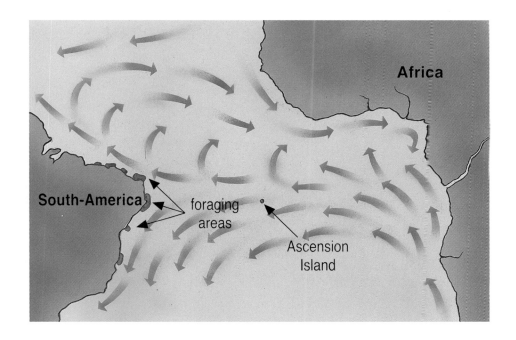

Green Turtle migration map from the island of Ascension to the Brazilian coast.
(Drawing: Tuvia Kurtz)

fall below 20°C. Adult female green turtles were marked when they came up to lay their eggs on the island of Ascension in the Atlantic Ocean. There are no food sources around the island, which is only 8 kilometers long. The closest feeding sites lie near the Brazilian coast about 2200 kilometers west of Ascension, where several of the marked females were found in due course. The turtles probably make use of sea currents in the Equatorial area to migrate these great distances to and from their breeding sites.

Among mammals, the flying mammals, bats, are unique in their migration. Many bats spend the winter hibernating in caves, where they can easily be trapped and marked. They are marked with numbered rings, similar to those used for ringing birds. Minute radio transmitters have also been attached to bats in order to track their migration routes. Among insectivorous bats in North America, some were found to migrate 500 kilometers north in spring, from their wintering sites. In another study, insectivorous bats marked in Russia were found 1000 kilometers from their wintering sites. Bats not only migrate to and from wintering sites, but do so during the winter as well, usually as a result of extreme weather changes that cause them to look for better caves to overwinter in. This migration is usually short, ranging no more than 150-200 kilometers. There are also bat species that perform distinct north-south migrations, similar to birds. One such case is the American insectivorous bat *Tadarida brasiliensis*. Every year, in spring, millions of females fly some 1500 kilometers north from winter quarters in Mexico to the southern United States (mainly Texas),

Migrating Green Turtle.
(Photo: Charles & Sandra Hood, Bruce Coleman Limited)

Page 32:
Salmon migrating upstream. (Photo: Alfred Limbrunner)

Bats hibernating in a cave.
(Photo: Alfred Limbrunner)

Page 35:
A Horseshoe Bat hibernating in a cave.
(Photo: Jens Rydell, Bruce Coleman Limited)

forming dense concentrations in caves where they give birth to their young. The advantage of this migration lies in the fact that the Mexican summer is hot and dry, so insects, their main food source, are not very active. The areas they migrate to, on the other hand, have an abundance of insects.

Some species of marine mammals, such as whales, are known for their long-distance migrations. One of these, the Humpback Whale, reaches a maximal length of 16 meters and weighs up to 40 tons, and is found both in the northern and southern hemispheres feeding mainly on fish and crustaceans. There are several distinct populations of Humpback Whale in different areas, including the coast of Antarctica, the northern Atlantic Ocean and the Pacific Ocean. In winter all these populations migrate towards the Equator where they inhabit the tropical seas, relatively close to the coast. Thus, whales that spend the summer in the Atlantic Ocean near Norway migrate south as winter approaches, to the western coast of Africa, having covered a distance close to 7000 kilometers. The population that spends the summers in the northeastern Pacific migrates south to the western coast of Mexico, more than 6000 kilometers away. The migration speed of Humpback Whales varies, but there are indications of individuals having covered distances of more than 100 kilometers in the space of one day!

The Blue Whale is the largest animal in existence, reaching a length of 33 meters and maximal weight of 130 tons. This species also migrates for very long distances. Populations from the northern Pacific migrate south to wintering areas in the Indian Ocean, up to the Gulf of Aden, a maximal distance of 13,000 kilometers. Other individuals spend the summer in the northern Atlantic Ocean and winter along the northwestern coast of Africa or in the southwestern Atlantic.

Among terrestrial mammals, the ungulates are famous for their mass migration. In the East African tropical region, three main species of ungulates migrate: Gnu, Zebra and Thomson's Gazelle. They leave the Serengeti plains in Tanzania and migrate north to the Masai-Mara plains in Kenya and back again. Their migration is seasonal and related to the rainfall regime in the area that influences the amount of food available to these ungulates. In this part of East Africa there are two rainy seasons, in winter and summer, and two dry seasons, in spring and autumn. During the autumn dry season the ungulate herds populate the Masai-Mara plains in southwestern Kenya where they enjoy plentiful grass that has grown following the summer rains. As winter rains draw near the herds migrate south to the Serengeti plains in Tanzania, where grass abounds following the rain, enabling these herbivores to survive the dry spring. As summer approaches the herds return north in the wake of summer rains, crossing the Mara River and returning once again to the Masai-Mara plains in Kenya. This migration follows a circular route that can reach 400 kilometers or more. Counts held show that the number of migrating Gnu (comprising the majority of this population), surpasses one million and is estimated at about 1,300,000. The number of Zebra and Thomson's Gazelle is significantly smaller. This mass migration provides a plentiful source of food for the carnivores in the East African savanna. Among these are lions that are able to prey on adult gnu and zebra. The Cheetah specializes in preying on Thomson's Gazelle. Some of these carnivores, such as the Spotted Hyena and the Hunting Dog will migrate in the wake of the ungulate herds, thus enjoying abundant food for relatively long periods of time.

Another mammal species undertaking mass migration is the Caribou. The Caribou inhabit the arctic areas in northern Europe, Asia and America, and some migrate seasonally according to the availability of food. The northern Canadian population of this species has the most renowned migration. Caribou spend the winter in relatively southern areas of northern Canada, west of the Hudson Bay. In winter, when a layer of ice covers the snow, the Caribou have difficulty locating the covered vegetation, their source of food. Some of them leave the tundra and migrate locally to the Spruce forests where the snow is deep but not covered by ice and dig in the snow with their legs to find food. In spring, between February and April, the Caribou herds begin moving towards their breeding grounds in the north. During this migration the herds may cover distances over 1000 kilometers in each direction. They cross rivers and water bodies whose temperature is only slightly above freezing, as well as high snow-covered mountains. They can cover up to 50 kilometers a day, in herds of

A lioness feeding on a Gnu hunted while on migration at the Masai-Mara Nature Reserve in Kenya.
(Photo: Ofer Bahat)

Humpback Whale - mother and young.
(Photo: J.D. Watt, Panda Photo)

Migrating Gnu herds on the Serengeti Plains in Tanzania.
(Photo: Eichhorn/Zingel, FLPA)

Reindeer migrating in norther Norway.
(Photo: Dr. Eckart Pott, Bruce Coleman Limited)

A beauty from the Boran tribe in northern Kenya.
(Photo: Yossi Leshem)

A Rendille warrior in northern Kenya.
(Photo: Yossi Leshem)

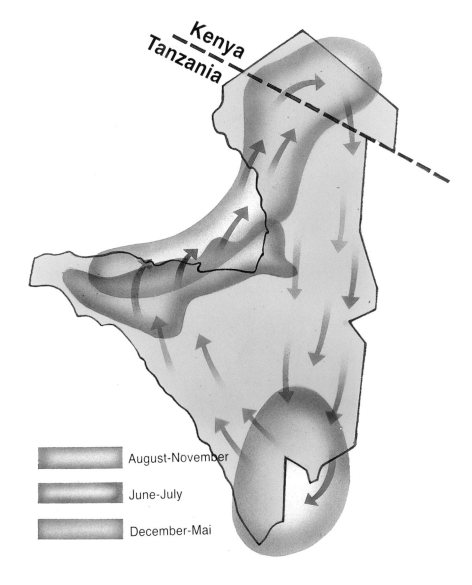

Kenya
Tanzania

August-November

June-July

December-Mai

The migration route taken by Gnu herds between the Serengeti Plains in Tanzania and the Masai-Mara Nature Reserve in Kenya. Between August and November the herds migrate to the northern part of the Serengeti Nature Reserve. Some of them cross the border north to the Masai-Mara Nature Reserve in Kenya (the upper part colored yellow on the map). Between May and December migration is towards the southern Serengeti (the lower part colored green on the map). During June and July Gnu herds concentrate in the southern and western part of the Serengeti Nature Reserve (the central part colored purple on the map).
(Drawing: Tuvia Kurtz)

hundreds of thousands, forming long lines of about 300 kilometers. The pregnant females lead the herd, giving birth shortly after reaching their breeding grounds.

Man has been characterized by an amazing migrating ability since ancient times. During pre-historic times man was a hunter and gatherer, migrating long distances to look for food and colonize new areas of the globe. *Australopithecus afarensis*, the earliest known precursor of man, inhabited Africa about 5 million years ago. The remains of the earliest prehistoric man that migrated outside Africa, *Homo erectus*, dating back about 300,000 years, were found in Southern Europe and Asia. Modern man, *Homo sapiens*, continued this migration and spread to other continents. About 30,000 years ago the first man reached the Australian continent, via the Indonesian Archipelago, crossing from island to island. Some 12,000 years later man had already spread over all of Australia. At this same time human migration in North America began. The Bering Strait was a land bridge in those days, and men coming from Siberia could cross east to what is today Alaska. The expansion of man south along the American Continent started along the western coast, continued down the center of the continent, and was aided by boats. Man reached the southern part of South America about 12,000 years ago.

During modern times humans migrate principally for purposes of immigration, using modern transportation methods that bring them from one end of the world to the next within a day. Migration is an integral part of the culture and life-style of nomadic communities in various parts of the world to this day, particularly those humans whose economy is based on grazing, who must migrate with their herds in search of food. One example of this are the thousands who migrate each year as summer approaches with domesticated Reindeer herds to grazing sites in the north of Lapland in northern Norway. In autumn they return south about 300 kilometers, to winter grazing sites in Finland, spending several months in each area. Another such case is found in the deserts of northern Kenya, where migration is an integral part of the life of several tribes. The Turkana tribe inhabits the area between the Turkana Lake in Northern Kenya and the Ugandan border to the west, and tribal economy is based on cattle, goats and camels. This area is extremely arid, so they must migrate with their herds to grazing grounds and to the few water holes in the area. The Turkana also have donkeys on which they load all their possessions during migration - including the wooden poles and tent materials. A typical family has four different types of herds, and they migrate about 25 times a year over an area that can range for 20,000 square miles!

Near the Turkana, southeast of the Turkana Lake, reside the Rendille. Their economy is based mainly on camels and they can cover distances up to 60 kilometers a day in search of food and water for them. The camels are extremely resistant to the dry conditions typical of the area and can survive without water up to ten days. They produce more milk than cattle and this is sometimes the only drinking source for the Rendille. Members of the Gabra tribe, who inhabit the area north of the Rendille also base their economy on camels, migrating great distances as well.

B. Bird Migration - Scope and Causes

Bird migration is undoubtedly the best known and most studied of all animal migrations. There are close to 9,000 different bird species in the world. Some are resident in one area during the whole year, others wander or migrate partially over short distances, and some are long-distance migrants. Partial migration is the situation in which part of the population of a given species is migratory with the remainder resident. In some cases only certain age groups, such as immature birds, migrate, while adults are resident. In others, males and females migrate at different times. Competition for food sources can cause some members of a given population to migrate in search of food. In total migration the entire population of a given species leaves its breeding quarters migrating great distances, usually thousands of kilometers to winter quarters.

The major factor determining migratory behavior in birds is food supply, which is in turn affected by seasonal weather changes. Birds in the Northern Hemisphere time their migration according to an invariable yearly occurrence: the shortening of the day. In other words, even if typical autumn weather is delayed and food is still available, the birds will not wait long for conditions to change, but set off on migration, in precise synchronization, triggered by the shortening of the day. In spring the same process takes place - birds in the Southern Hemisphere react to the diminishing day length and begin migrating north.

Bird migration patterns have evolved over millions of years. Even now, these patterns are not rigid, but change frequently according to weather conditions, food availability and a variety of other factors. Migration between the northern and southern hemispheres involves many dangers for birds. One frequently asked question is why do birds migrate at all, instead of remaining all year in the tropics? The answer is fairly simple - there is an abundance of food in the Northern Hemisphere in summer. If northern birds would not return to their breeding grounds in spring, the vast amounts of food available there would be wasted. In the tropics weather conditions are more or less stable throughout the year, providing relatively abundant food sources for birds. This results in high population densities and fierce competition for food. The resident birds of the area are well adapted to the ecological niches to which they occupy and can compete better for food than visiting birds from the north. This has led to "leap-frog migration" in which some of the migrating birds from the north skip over the tropics, flying on to winter quarters in the southern hemisphere where there is less competition.

Basic migration patterns probably started evolving in the ancestors of modern birds. About 150 million years ago the land mass of Pangaea split into two major continents - Laurasia and Gondwana - and the birds had to find a way to move

The Bluethroat breeds in the Arctic Circle and migrates south as winter approaches.
(Photo: Ofer Bahat)

Starlings winter in giant flocks of one to five million individuals!
(Photo: Graham Burns, The Environmental Picture Library)

The Kestrel is resident in most of its breeding areas in Europe and hunts its prey even in the snow.
(Photo: Alfred Limbrunner)

between the two parts. Approximately 100 million years ago India drifted away from the southern end of Gondwana and began moving north. The location of Europe, Asia and Africa was very similar to their present location. North and South America however, were still separate and very far apart. North America was attached to Europe as part of the Laurasian continent. Most of the antecedents of modern bird species developed during this period. Continental drift had a major influence on species diversity. Examples of this can be found in the composition of North American passerines: research has shown that there are more passerine species common to North America and Europe than to North and South America. In other words, North America and Europe have more in common, probably as a result of the ancient link between the land masses that existed at the time the ancestors of modern species evolved. Continental drift also affected the pattern of bird migration from the Northern Hemisphere southwards. There is extensive migration between Europe and Asia to Africa, which is explained by the ancient connection that existed between them. Migration between North and South America, on the other hand, is much smaller, probably as a result of the great distance between them in the past up to about 10 million years ago.

Despite all the above the effect of continental drift is gradual and cumulative, since the process occurred (and still does), slowly, over millions of years. Changes in climate have a rapid and immediate effect on bird movements. At a relatively late stage ice ages had a significant effect on migratory patterns. The glaciers in Europe, Asia and North America moved northwards and southwards, in an identical pattern, during the Pleistocene (2 million - 10,000 years ago). The birds too, moved north and south, as they followed the glaciers' advance and retreat. This pattern reinforced existing migration movements caused by seasonal weather changes and fluctuations in food availability.

In light of all these, a migratory pattern developed in which a huge mass of birds from the Northern Hemisphere moves to winter quarters in the south each year, and back again. The distance covered in these migrations varies between different species. A relatively small number of species does not migrate at all, but spends the winter in their breeding quarters, actually staying in the same area all year round. These birds possess adaptations that allow them to find food and spend the winter in the north. Other species migrate for short distances in order to spend the winter in more comfortable surroundings. The remaining species are long-distance migrants that reach the tropics, with some flying even further south to winter in the Southern Hemisphere.

Birds are generally associated with their breeding areas, even though some spend very little time there. One such example is the Honey Buzzard that breeds in Europe and western Asia. The Honey Buzzard returns to its breeding quarters towards the end of May. It completes the nesting process in less than three months and cares for its young. By the end of August the Honey Buzzard is once again on its way back to winter quarters in Africa. Although they spend only about 3 months in their breeding quarters, Honey Buzzards, by definition, belong to an Asian or European population. This species, which feeds mainly on bees and wasps, must migrate south for winter, as their food is unavailable in the Northern Hemisphere where winter temperatures can descend below zero. At these low temperatures bees and wasps are not active, so that the Honey Buzzard does not have on what to feed in its breeding quarters.

Research using various methods such as ringing (banding), field observations, location by radar and more (as will be described in forthcoming chapters), has provided extensive and interesting data on bird migration, with emphasis on migratory ranges and speed.

Small passerines, whose body mass does not exceed 10-20 grams, migrate great distances in many cases. The Arctic Warbler, whose body length is about 12 centimeters and weighs a mere 10 grams, breeds in the northernmost parts of Scandinavia and Russia. It flies from breeding areas to winter quarters in Southeast Asia, covering distances up to 12,500 kilometers in each direction during its migration.

The Wheatear whose body length is only about 15 centimeters breeds in various European locations, including some far north beyond the Arctic Circle, in Iceland,

The Chaffinch migrates south from its breeding quarters in northern Europe as far as Africa.
(Photo: Ofer Bahat)

Page 47:
A Honey Buzzard in its nest holding a wasp comb in its claws.
(Photo: Alfred Limbrunner)

A male Wheatear.
(Photo: Michael McKavett, Bruce Coleman Limited)

Wheatear migration map from its breeding grounds (red) to its winter quarters (green).
(Drawing: Tuvia Kurtz)

Greenland and east to Siberia. It has also spread to Northeast Canada and to Alaska. This Wheatear migrates south in autumn to winter in the semi-arid Sahel in Africa south of the Sahara, and to the savannas further south. The population that spread via Greenland to Eastern Canada migrates to winter quarters, east across Greenland, and south across Europe to Africa. The Wheatear population that spread from Siberia across the Bering Strait to Alaska also flies back and crosses the entire Asian continent on its way to Africa. This long-distance migration can span over 15,000 kilometers in each direction. In other words, Wheatears fly more than 30,000 kilometers a year, in some cases, on their journey from northern breeding quarters to wintering grounds in Africa!

The Arctic Tern is undoubtedly the champion long-distance migrant among birds. This tern, a seabird feeding principally on small fish, breeds in the Arctic Circle in the north and winters in the Southern Hemisphere, as far south as Antarctica. The terns appear to migrate from breeding to winter quarters along the coastline - that is, not in a straight line. They cover an average of 20,000 kilometers in each direction, and during one year will fly up to 40,000 kilometers, a distance equaling the circumference of the earth at the Equator!!

Other sea birds too have characteristically long migration routes. The Manx Shearwater population that breeds on the coast of the British Isles, Ireland and Iceland migrates south to the eastern coast of South America. The adult shearwaters abandon

An Arctic Tern.
(Photo: Alfred Limbrunner)

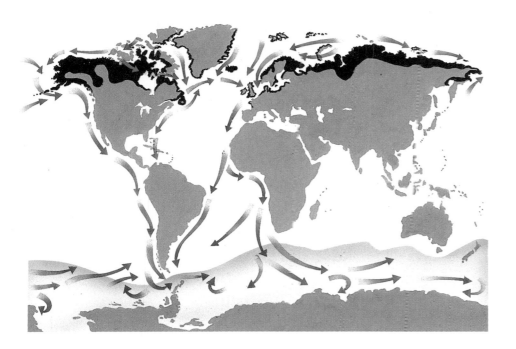

Arctic Tern migration map, the "world record holder" that covers 40,000 kilometers yearly on migration (a distance equal to the circumference of the globe), from breeding quarters in the Northern Hemisphere (purple) to winter quarters in the Southern Hemisphere (blue).
(Drawing: Tuvia Kurtz)

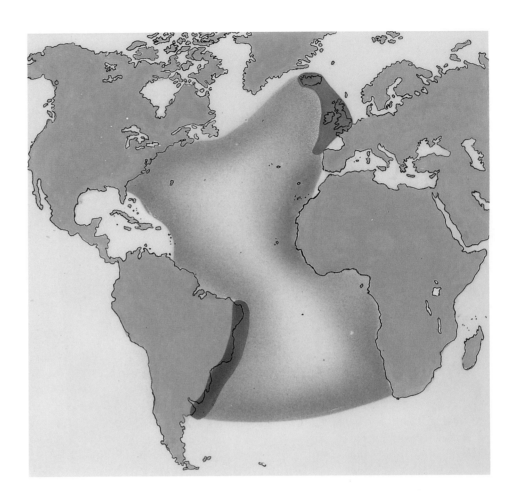

Manx Shearwater migration map from its breeding quarters in northwestern Europe (purple) to its winter quarters in South America (red).
(Drawing: Tuvia Kurtz)

The Gannet is a sea bird breeding on islands in the Northern Hemisphere and wintering on the oceans and even in the Mediterranean.
(Photo: Ofer Bahat)

their young at the end of August and immediately begin migrating south. The young, when they realize their parents will not return, quickly fly off and migrate in the wake of the adults. One young Manx Shearwater ringed at its nest in Wales in western Britain, was found dead on the shores of Brazil, only 17 days after it was ringed. Assuming it left its nest on the day it was ringed, and that it flew in a straight line, this young shearwater flew at least 7,200 kilometers on its first flight south, a daily distance surpassing 400 kilometers!

The Short-tailed Shearwater breeds on the southeastern coast of Australia and on the Tasmanian coast. It leaves its breeding grounds in the beginning of spring and flies north, wandering and feeding for seven months along the coast of Eastern Asia, to the waters of Alaska, and then south along the western coast of North America, back to its breeding quarters. The total distance this species covers can reach 32,000 kilometers!!! The shearwaters exploit winds blowing over the Pacific Ocean in order to preserve energy for flying.

The Steppe Eagle that passes over the Eilat Mountains in southern Israel during migration flies an average of 20,000 kilometers while migrating from Asia to Africa and back. Its life span can reach 25 years, which means that during a lifetime it flies an average of 500,000 kilometers just while migrating!

Movements of birds from breeding to winter quarters are not always south and can sometimes be in the opposite direction. The Puffin, a conspicuously colored bird similar to penguins, is found in the northern part of the Atlantic Ocean (as opposed to penguins found only south of the tropics). Puffins ringed at the nest in the British Isles in summer were found in winter, in Greenland, among other sites, at least 2,000 kilometers away in a northwesterly direction. Since they feed on fish, they do not necessarily migrate south, but also north where fish are abundant in winter.

Birds must complete their migration as an accurately timed, synchronized part of their yearly activity. Various factors can cause changes in the elements of a bird's yearly cycle and birds have developed different strategies to deal with this situation. These are determined both by evolutionary development, originating from stable factors and by circumstantial changes in field conditions, as illustrated by the following examples. By arriving early at breeding quarters a bird can occupy preferred nesting territories and have more time to complete its nesting cycle. But early arrival also has risks, since if the weather is still cold there is little food available, and those birds nesting early may begin in less than optimal body conditions. Birds completing the process of nesting and raising young rapidly can undertake an additional breeding cycle. This is vital when a first nesting attempt has failed, and even when not, makes it possible for some species to produce more young. On the other hand, if less time is spent on caring for young, parents have less time to teach and train them. Extended parental care also has the advantage of improving the physical condition of young birds that have little experience in finding food. Early departure from breeding sites south allows birds to avoid cold weather that sometimes arrives earlier than expected. On the other hand, it prevents them from fully exploiting food sources available at breeding sites. Some species stopover many times during their migratory journey, while others migrate almost continuously. The advantage of the first strategy is that the birds using it do not need to store fat, since they feed along the way. Its disadvantage lies in the fact that food is not always readily available along the migration route and fat accumulation is insurance against such cases.

From all these we see that migration is not only an important element in a bird's yearly activity cycle, but actually is the major factor which determines other phases in this cycle. In view of all the above many scientists have attempted to estimate migration mass: the number of individuals of each species, and the total number of individuals that undertake migration. Moreau, a British ornithologist who spent many years of his life studying bird migration between Europe and Asia to Africa, estimated the total number of birds migrating to Africa at 3.75 billion!!! This count includes only songbirds and other terrestrial birds, and does not include waterfowl. According to Moreau the estimated numbers of migrants for some species are Willow Warbler - 900 million, Sand Martin - 375 million, Tree Pipit - 260 million, Spotted Flycatcher - 250 million and Barn Swallow - 220 million. Moreau also estimated that an additional 200 million small non-passerines (mainly swifts) migrate and 40 million birds of prey (mainly falcons). These estimates are based on population densities in breeding areas and on the size of these areas. It is difficult to verify these claims, especially for passerines and other small birds that are hard to locate and count, but the order of magnitude is probably correct. If we add the birds that migrate from eastern Asia to the southern end of the continent, and those that migrate between North and South America, there are undoubtedly thousands of millions of birds that migrate yearly over most of the globe.

A Puffin with a bill-full of eels.
(Photo: Ofer Bahat)

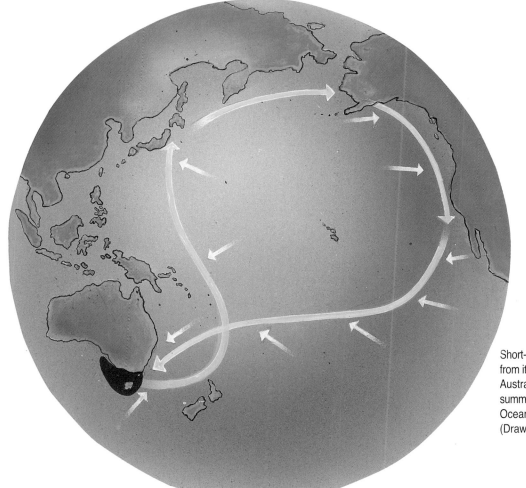

Short-tailed Shearwater migration map from its breeding quarters in southeast Australia and Tasmania (red) to its summer quarters in the northern Pacific Ocean.
(Drawing: Tuvia Kurtz)

51

C. How Bird Flight Principles are Applied in Migration

Lift When birds fly, their wings seem to push the air down and back, so the bird rises and flies forward. This impression is mistaken, since in reality the bird does not displace air in order to fly, but moves its wing forward allowing air to flow over the wing from back to front creating lift. The backward movement of the wing takes place at an angle that produces minimal resistance and its return forwards creates renewed lift.

Lift production is based primarily on wing structure (which is similar in birds and aircraft): a section of a bird wing shows that it is not flat, but convex on the upper side, and concave on the lower. Thus, the anterior edge of the wing (the leading edge) is thicker, and the posterior part (the trailing edge) is thinner. When an air current hits the leading edge of the wing, it divides, part of it flowing over the wing and part of it under it. The air flowing above the wing has a longer distance to pass within a given time unit than the air flowing under it and so flows faster, creating a pressure loss above the wing. The air passing under the wing has a shorter distance to cover, thus flowing faster, creating greater pressure. The pressure difference is directed downward, producing an upward force termed "lift".

The magnitude of lift depends on the pressure difference: the more convex the wing the greater the difference, to the point where the wing angle is so great that continuous air flow over the wing is impeded. This causes loss of lift and results in stalling. Another important force affecting the wing is "drag": the force that resists flight progress. This force pulls backwards, in the same direction as wind flow and opposite to the direction of the bird's flight. One drag producing factor is the air in the high pressure area below the wing, which flows backwards in the direction of the low pressure area above. As a result turbulence is created, which passes over the leading edge of the wing to its tip. Lift increases with flight speed, so that reducing drag to a minimum greatly increases the efficiency of bird flight.

Additional drag is created from air flowing over the bird's body. In order to reduce it the bird must have an optimal aerodynamic structure, particularly in high-speed flight.

The relation between lift and drag expresses the true force acting on the wing. When lift is ten times stronger than drag, the lift:drag ratio is said to be 10:1. Birds need as high as possible a lift:drag ratio. The ratio is enhanced in a body and wings with improved aerodynamic structure. Nevertheless, the control the bird has over the angle at which the wing is held in relation to the air current is of major importance. This angle is called the angle of attack or angle of incidence. The larger the angle of attack, the greater lift is. However, above a certain critical angle, usually between 12 and 16 degrees, continuous airflow over the wing ceases, and stalling occurs. In this situation lift is canceled while drag increases significantly. The bird, therefore, must fly at an angle of attack which provides a high lift:drag ratio and will not cause it to stall. These conditions are usually attained at an angle of attack of three to four degrees.

The wing has two other major characteristics: wing loading and wing aspect ratio. Wing loading is the ratio between the weight of the bird (or aircraft) to its wing area. The higher wing loading is, the faster the bird has to fly in order to create sufficient lift for flying. The wing aspect ratio is the ratio between wing length (wingspan) and wing breadth (wing chord). A long, narrow wing has a higher wing aspect ratio than a short, broad wing. A long, narrow wing produces little drag, as it has a large area for creating lift, but it has a narrow tip that creates some turbulence. These traits provide good gliding ability. Minimal drag is the main advantage of a wing with a high wing aspect ratio. However, such a wing that is long and narrow has a relatively weak structure which is not resistant to sharp aerobatic maneuvers. Birds or planes that maneuver sharply have relatively short wings, with a low wing aspect ratio.

Birds use several types of flight and can combine them, according to conditions in the field and body structure. The main types of flight used by birds are gliding and flapping.

Page 52:
A Barn Swallow flying from its nest.
(Photo: Eric and David Hosking, FLPA)

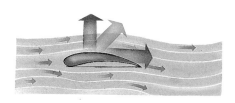

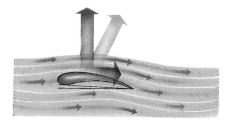

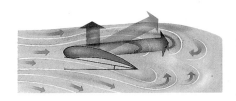

Airflow over the surface of an aerodynamic wing creates lift and drag. The ratio between the magnitude of these forces is dependent on the wing's angle of attack: when the wing is completely horizontal (angle of attack = 0, upper drawing), lift and drag forces are weak. Raising the angle of attack causes lift to increase to its maximal value (at an angle of attack of about 5 degrees) and drag to decrease (middle drawing). When the angle of attack is even higher - drag increases rapidly, until when the angle of attack is about 15 degrees, stalling occurs - there is no lift and drag increases to its maximal value.
(Drawings: Tuvia Kurtz)

Gliding flight   In gliding flight the bird uses gravity as the propelling force, just as a bicycle rider rides passively down a road, thus overcoming the drag that pulls it back. Gliding occurs at a speed high enough to create sufficient lift for the bird to stay airborne. If there were no drag, a bird could glide forward without losing altitude. However, since drag slows the bird's progress, it loses altitude continuously while gliding.

The glide ratio is the relationship between the horizontal distance the bird covers while gliding, and the vertical distance it covers in that same time unit (or alternatively its altitude loss). In order to extend the glide as long as possible the bird tries to decrease its glide angle (the angle between the horizontal to the angle of actual flight), thus decreasing its sink rate (rate of altitude loss). The bird therefore holds it wings at an angle of attack that can provide an optimal lift:drag ratio. Slow flight helps, but if it is too slow it can cause stalling, The bird must thus fly at a velocity in which drag is minimal, glide ratio optimal and there is no danger of stalling.

The advantage a bird has over an aircraft with a rigid wing is that it can flex its wings at any angle it chooses, adapting its aerodynamic shape to its needs. In gliding flight the shift in wing angle is of enormous advantage, since it allows the bird to preserve an optimal lift:drag ratio and minimal gliding angle over a large range of flight speeds. Spread wings have a maximal area, and in this situation wing loading decreases and with it the sink rate. Closed wings have the opposite effect. When a bird wants to increase its gliding velocity (and sink rate), it closes its wings partially, so that the wing extremity (from the wing joint outwards) bends back, and the primary feathers overlap forming a sharp tip. As a result, gliding speed can increase doubly or more. Birds will exploit this feature when hunting or preparing to land, for example.

Birds with long wings glide extremely efficiently as a result of their ability to vary the angle of attack of different wing sections. In some cases the inner wing angle of attack is high, while the outer part (from the wing joint out) is turned on its axis and held at an angle of attack of zero (horizontal) or even slanted down. The bird can thus efficiently control wing area, air flow over the wing and the lift:drag ratio. It can then glide at very low speeds, at which an aircraft, whose wings are rigid, would stall.

Opening the alula at high angles of attack prevents turbulence and stalling. (Drawing: Tuvia Kurtz)

Another means by which birds use to avoid stalling is the bastard wing (alula): it is composed of 3 or 4 very short feathers, attached to the leading edge of the wing at the end of the "arm". These feathers can move from the leading edge upwards. When the angle of attack is too great, the wing stalls, since continuous airflow above it is interrupted, resulting in turbulence. By opening the alula continuous airflow is maintained even at very high angles of attack that would otherwise cause stalling. At high angles of attack the alula opens automatically, due to low pressure created in the leading edge area that causes its feathers to move upwards. Airplane wings have leading edge slats that perform exactly like the alula during landing, in order to prevent stalling.

Another important property of bird wings is the bird's ability to open its primary feathers in a manner similar to spread fingers. These feathers are asymmetrical: the anterior part (that faces the flight direction) is narrower than the posterior part. Each flight feather has a notch at the tip of its inner web. This lessens the drag produced by each primary, reducing the gliding bird's sink rate and postponing the necessity of shifting to flapping flight. In addition each flight feather behaves as a separate airfoil that can change its angle in relation to the air flowing around the bird. When the total wing angle of attack is very high, and could cause stalling, the primary feathers are held at a lower angle of attack that still allows lift production, thus raising the value of the angle of attack at which stalling occurs.

The bird's tail plays an important role in intensifying lift. When spread, it acts as a broad surface that improves lift. In certain birds of prey tail expansion can reduce wing load by about 20%. The tail is also important in enhancing air flow over the wings at low flight speeds: the spread tail acts as an extension of the wing surface, sustaining the smooth air flow from the wing's leading edge backwards, without creating turbulence at high angles of attack - particularly during take-off and landing. This is most obvious in birds with a high aspect ratio that fly relatively slowly while searching for food, such as swallows, kites and terns. All these have sharply forked

Scops Owl in flight - wing beat sequence.
(Photo: Panda Photo)

Pages 56-57:
A male Kestrel in flight compared to an F-15 fighter plane (called a "falcon" in the Israel Air Force).
(Kestrel photo: Kim Taylor, Bruce Coleman Limited, F-15 photo: courtesy of the Israel Air Force)

leading edge

air inlet

vertical stabilizer

trailing edge

leading edge

alula

primaries

trailing edge

rectrices

Broad-billed Hummingbird sipping nectar.
(Photo: Bob & Clara Calhoun, Bruce Coleman Limited)

tails - with the outer rectrices longer than the inner ones. This type of tail increases lift at low speeds, improving the smooth flow of air and preventing stalling at high angles of attack. Another important function of the tail is as a rudder for steering and stabilization.

Flapping flight   This is the most common flight method in many birds and is used mainly by small birds, while large birds prefer gliding. Flapping flight provides lift for remaining airborne and propulsion for moving forwards. The number of wing beats per second is a measure of the bird's speed, but this number depends mainly on wing loading and the type of flight. The Grey Heron, a large bird, has about 2 wing beats a second. The Herring Gull has an average of 2.8 wing beats a second, the Pheasant 9 beats a second, the Great Tit about 25, and hummingbirds, the smallest birds can hover like a helicopter in one place, beating their wings 80 times a second!

A bird expends great amounts of energy in flight, and among the close to 9,000 species known today about 40 have completely lost the ability to fly, such as penguins. Other birds, such as the various game birds, do not fly a lot, doing so usually only to escape predators. Flapping flight is the most energy expensive, so the heavier a bird is the harder it is for it to fly actively. In flapping flight a bird expends 20 times more energy than in gliding and soaring flight.

Bird Weight and Wing Structure   There is an upper limit to the body mass of flying birds. Birds weighing more than about 15 kilograms cannot fly. Some birds whose body mass is close to this value are the Californian Condor, the Andean Condor and the Kori Bustard. The Californian Condor flies by soaring and gliding and does not use flapping flight, while the Bustard rarely flies, and even then only for short distances.

Relatively large, heavy birds, such as raptors, usually glide at great speed in order to increase the lift created by air passing over the wing. By doing so they save energy needed to create lift, and rarely use flapping flight.

Wing structure has a marked influence on the type of flight a bird uses, and consequently on its life style. A combination of a relatively broad wing that reduces wing load and a long wing that minimizes drag, are of major advantage for birds that use mainly flapping flight. This type of wing however, is suitable only for birds living and active in open spaces. Long wings are mechanically weaker, and do not allow tight maneuvers, vital for birds living in dense woods. As a result, wing structure is actually a compromise between pure aerodynamic considerations and the conditions of the area inhabited by the bird. This is illustrated in the following table:

Female Kestrel diving with open alulas. (Photo: Ofer Bahat)

Species	Typical habitat	Wing load	Aspect ratio (gram/cm^2)	Stalling velocity (km/h)
Wren	woodland	0.24	6.9	18.4
Kestrel	open spaces	0.35	7.7	22.3
Dove	woodland	0.52	6.3	27.3
Mallard	water	1.20	9.0	41.4
Albatross	oceans	1.37	18.7	44.3

Use of Thermals   One of the most efficient methods of saving energy is the use of air currents that provide the bird with extra lift. This is optimally achieved by flying using a combination of soaring and gliding. Soaring is based on the use of rising air currents that allow the bird to proceed by gliding for long distances, expending little energy on maintaining flight altitude. When wind strikes a salient topographical object, such as a mountain range or high cliff, it breaks in different directions. A substantial portion of the new air currents usually rises and is used by birds for soaring. Some birds, such as raptors, regularly exploit these obstruction currents. They receive the needed lift from the air current and glide progressively without losing altitude.

Pelicans soaring in a thermal.
(Photo: Ofer Bahat)

Migrating storks circling in a thermal while gaining altitude.
(Photo: Ofer Bahat)

Updrafts are also created as a result of the hot surface of the earth. When the sun warms the ground the adjacent cold air warms up. The lighter warm air rises as a bubble, called a thermal, that can be depicted as a turbulence turning on its axis. The air current rises in the center of the thermal rapidly and spreads to the sides when it reaches the top of the bubble.

Thermals are formed over areas that heat up more than their surroundings, such as rock surfaces, dry sand or a clearing in the woods. When the thermal rises through colder air its humidity can condense and form a cloud. This is characteristic of clear, warm days. When winds, such as a breeze from the sea, blow, a series of thermals, formed in the same place, drift with the wind, each with its own cloud, forming a "corridor" of thermals. Each thermal eventually reaches a maximal altitude above which it does not rise. Thermals are formed in the morning, when the sun is at an angle high enough to warm the ground efficiently. They stop forming in the afternoon, as the sun sets and the ground cools.

Thermals are not formed above the sea, although in tropical areas the sea sometimes heats up excessively and warm air currents, that birds use for soaring, are formed.

The goal of gliding birds (and glider pilots) is to locate a thermal and soar with it. In order to use the thermal for lift the bird must soar circularly within the thermal bubble, as close as possible to its center where the strongest upwinds occur. A bird gliding with flexed wings, wing and tail feathers closed, changes its flight when entering a thermal: it slows down, spreads its wings, opens its primaries and spreads its tail. By doing so the bird reduces the rate of descent to a minimum and increases its lift surface to a maximum.

The flight behavior of a soaring bird is largely dependent on the force of the thermal. The bird can control its rate of ascent by changing its location in relation to the thermal center. When a soaring bird is within the thermal bubble it expends minimal energy and rises to altitudes from which it can glide at any time in a chosen direction.

Large, heavy birds, with relatively broad wings, such as vultures, storks and pelicans, are usually dependent on thermals for their flight. These birds use thermals both for foraging and wandering around their territory and for migrating long distances between continents.

Flight in formation and exploitation of wing shape   Many flocking birds commonly fly in V-type formation. This is not incidental since it provides the birds with a distinct aerodynamic advantage. When a bird flies, turbulence, moving backwards, is created at its wing-tips. A bird flying behind the wing tips of another exploits this turbulence in order to enhance lift and reduce the energy needed for flight. According to this principle the bird leading the formation does not benefit from increased lift. As a result, changing places in the formation while flying is important for the lead bird so it too, can benefit from the advantages of V-formation flight.

Thermals are formed as the ground is warmed by the sun's rays. The warm air current rises upwards and dissolves as the air cools at higher altitudes. (Drawing: Tuvia Kurtz)

Migrating birds apply flight principles in a manner adapted in the best possible way to their aerodynamic traits and to the environmental conditions they encounter on migration. Wing shape is of great importance for long-distance migratory flight. Small passerines usually have short, somewhat rounded wings with a low aspect ratio, but relatively large area. As a result their wing loading is low and they can afford to increase their body weight significantly by accumulating fat, which they store as an energy reserve for migration.

The disadvantage of a broad wing is the drag it creates. Small passerines often overcome this problem by using undulating flight, in which they rise by flapping open wings and then glide with folded wings, held close to the body. Gliding with closed wings significantly reduces drag.

Many long-distance migrants have a characteristic long, narrow wing, with reduced drag. In species of the same genus, such as the *Sylvia* warblers, the long-distance migrant species have longer, narrower wings than related species that migrate short distances. Differences in wing dimensions can even be found in different populations of the same species: Blackcaps from Northern Europe that migrate to Africa have longer, narrower wings than the resident Blackcaps of Southern Europe.

High-altitude flight Studies done with radar in different parts of the world show that birds sometimes fly at extremely high altitudes, up to several kilometers above sea-level. Small birds (probably passerines) were located by radar flying over Puerto Rico at an altitude of 6.8 kilometers. At this altitude air pressure is half that at sea level and air temperature 12 degrees Celsius below zero. The advantage of high-altitude flight lies in the avoidance of strong, unstable winds, sandstorms and other weather hazards typical of lower elevations. There is also an advantage to very strong, but stable winds, at high altitudes, that birds can use to their benefit. Low temperatures are beneficial since they prevent overheating resulting from the exertion of flying.

Most birds migrate at a maximal altitude of 1.5 kilometers. The minority migrates at higher altitudes, usually up to 5 kilometers. During the past few years, however bird migration has been found at much higher altitudes - as far as 12 kilometers (!!!) above sea level.

Pelicans gliding out from a thermal in V-formation. The photo was taken from the motorized glider over the western Negev.
(Photo: Yossi Leshem)

Cranes flying in V-formation.
(Photo: Roland Mayr)

Geese and Cranes have been observed migrating across the Himalayas at altitudes of 29,000 feet (about 9 kilometers).

On 29 November 1973 a passenger plane collided with a bird over the Ivory Coast in West Africa. The collision occurred at an altitude of 37,000 feet (12.3 kilometers)!!! The pilot was forced to land because one of the engines had been hit. The feather remains in the engine were examined and found to belong to a Ruppel's Griffon Vulture (a vulture found in various parts of Africa, and sometimes seen in southern Sinai and the Arabian Peninsula). This is apparently the highest altitude any bird has been discovered at.

On 9 December 1967 at about 3:00 P.M., a radar operator in Northern Ireland detected a powerful echo moving southwards at an altitude of about 8 kilometers. He made radio-contact with a pilot flying in the vicinity and the pilot reported a flock of about 30 swans flying at an altitude of 8.2 kilometers. The swans were migrating between Iceland and Ireland. Their flight speed was measured and found to be 180 kilometers per hour!!! Assuming this was their average flight speed, the swans covered the 1,200 kilometers between Iceland and Ireland in less than 7 hours!!!

Air temperature drops by 1°C for every 150 meters of increasing altitude. At an altitude of 8 kilometers ambient temperature can go as low as 40°C below zero. At this altitude the partial pressure of oxygen is about a third of its value at sea level and human beings need a supply of pure oxygen in order to survive.

It would seem to be impossible to migrate at these altitudes. However, the structure of the avian respiratory system that includes in addition to the lungs, a network of 9 connected air sacs, allows birds to fly and be active at altitudes in which mammals cannot survive. The activity of the bird's strong flight muscles creates large amounts of heat and probably helps them regulate their body temperature even at altitudes where ambient temperature is very low. Wing movements in flight, and the air sacs have a significant effect on the respiratory process in birds. When wings are raised, the air sacs inflate and air from the lungs flows into them. When the wings are lowered, the air sacs deflate, and the air in them flows out through the lungs. Although there is almost no gas exchange in the air sacs, they serve as air reservoirs: air passes through the lungs into the air sacs and its oxygen is absorbed once. When it leaves the air sacs it passes through the lungs again and oxygen is absorbed a second time. The avian respiratory system thus extracts oxygen from the air much more efficiently than the mammalian respiratory system.

Birds regularly flying at high altitudes have developed another characteristic that helps them breathe efficiently. The Bar-headed Goose, for example, crosses the Himalayas twice a year while migrating from its breeding quarters in Siberia to winter quarters in India. Studies have shown that the hemoglobin in its blood binds oxygen significantly better than other goose species that do not have to fly so high. This trait found in other high-altitude flying birds such as Ruppel's Griffon Vulture, is of considerable importance for absorbing oxygen from the air at altitudes where its pressure is very low.

At high altitudes (5 kilometers and above), jet streams, air currents that move extremely fast (150-200 kilometers per hour), are found. Birds reaching this altitude can progress at speeds three and four times as great as their average flight velocity at low altitudes. Some of the migrating birds seem to know how to exploit jet streams in order to fly at great speeds. However, there are still many questions about high-altitude migration that remain unanswered and much to be studied about this fascinating subject.

The limiting factors for high-altitude flight in birds are low ambient temperatures and low oxygen concentrations in the air. Therefore, air currents permitting, birds prefer in many cases to fly at high altitudes, as far up as ambient temperature and oxygen concentration allow.

Weather has a significant effect on migrating birds. Even if migrating birds have stored enough energy for the journey they are subject to winds, rain and other factors, that can deflect them from their migratory route and confound prior energy calculations. Migrating birds frequently use tail winds that help them progress and save energy. Tail winds allow them to invest less energy in flapping flight, while preserving the

Bar-headed Geese cross the Himalayas twice a year during migration.
(Photo: Ofer Bahat)

Jet height migration

The Israel Air Force has recorded several instances where birds were found migrating at extreme altitudes:

On 30 April 1987, at the peak of spring migration, Colonel N, a F-15 wing commander, was flying at an altitude of 20,000 feet (about 6.1 kilometers), in the Mitzpe-Ramon area (southern Israel). He noticed several dozen large birds flying in the vicinity and identified them as birds of prey, although this identification was not verified.

On 22 September 1988, at the height of autumn migration, Israel Air Force ground control units picked up unidentified movements at an altitude of 24,000 feet (7.3 kilometers), in an area about 9 kilometers south of the Dead Sea. Captain A, one of the fighter pilots sent out to the unknown target, identified a flock of about 200 light colored birds of undetermined species, migrating south in V-formation.

In March 1990, during spring migration, a F-16 fighter aircraft collided with an unidentified bird over the Mediterranean while flying along the coast at an altitude of 28,000 feet (about 8.5 kilometers)!! The plane suffered no significant damage, but bird bloodstains were found on it.

On 24 September 1990, at the peak of autumn migration, Lieutenant G was flying a Phantom on a training flight at an altitude of 20,000 feet. At 11:40 A.M. a flock of about 150 white birds "the size of gulls" (in the pilot's words), flew over 2000 feet above him (at an altitude of about 6.7 kilometers!). The birds were flying in two V-formations, one large and one smaller. This occurred only two years and two days after the incident in the southern Dead Sea.

On 29 January 1994, during the noon hours, the Israel Air Force Ground Control Unit discovered a unidentified target which entered Israeli air space from Sinai at an altitude of 15,000 feet (about 4.5 kilometers) and a speed of 150 knots (273 kilometers per hour). Fighter aircraft were scrambled and made eye contact from a range of about 100 meters. From the debriefing of one of the pilots, Major Y, the target was found to be a flock of dark birds that the pilot identified as ducks, flying actively in V-formation. When the fighter aircraft approached them at a distance of about 100 meters, the ducks dispersed in fright, but the minute the plane passed they reorganized in an echelon formation. Information received from the Air Force Meteorological Unit, showed that there was a strong, high altitude jet stream in the area at that time. This jet stream apparently allowed the ducks to progress at the amazing velocity of 273 kilometers per hour, about four times their normal flight speed at low altitudes!! Other flocks were also located by ground control units on similar flight routes and altitudes that night and the day after!

An F-15 fighter plane climbing vertically on a high-altitude flight over the Israeli coast.
(Photo: Gil Arbel, The Israel Air Force Magazine)

same ground speed, or to fly at higher ground speeds than would be possible without tail winds.

Migration flight strategies   Migrating birds can be divided into two major groups: those using active flapping flight and those using soaring and gliding (passive flight). The basis of this distinction lies in the fundamental difference between small and large birds. With the increase in size, a bird's weight is cubed, while its wing area is only squared. As a result, the heavier a bird, the more difficult it is for it to create lift in active flight by using its wings alone. The transition from one group to another is not marked, but gradual, from small active flyers to larger gliders, that can reach a weight of about 15 kilograms. Most birds belong to the first group, including passerines, waders, and many others. These birds fly by flapping their wings rapidly for hours on end during migration. They are also called "ocean-

A Lanner Falcon turning sharply to the left with a "last look" at the photographer.
(Photo: Eyal Bartov)

Page 69:
The Robin is one of the hundreds of species migrating at night using flapping flight.
(Photo: Kim Taylor, Bruce Coleman Limited)

crossers" since they can cross large bodies of water (such as the Mediterranean) in continuous active flight, never stopping to rest. Quails are one of the outstanding illustrations of this type of migration. They gather in southern Turkey, in the southern Aegean Peninsula and in southern Italy before migrating. As darkness descends they leave on their journey and cross the Mediterranean in one night of continuous flying.

Soaring birds do not cross large water bodies such as the Mediterranean, during migration, but circumvent them, since no thermals form above them. Raptors (large species) and other soaring birds have good reason to lengthen their migration journey by hundreds of kilometers. The detour saves significant amounts of energy, since they can soar and glide over land. Their dependence on thermals increases migration time for soaring birds since thermals are formed only in the daytime, therefore limiting migration to daylight hours.

The differences between small, actively flying birds and large, soaring and gliding birds can be summarized in the following manner: the former migrate during both day and night, along direct, relatively short routes, from breeding grounds to winter quarters. They migrate over the sea, on a broad front, and do not converge into distinct migration routes. Since they expend great amounts of energy for migration they must store fat before leaving on their journey. Most of them migrate at night, when dangers of predation are reduced and heat load is lower, facilitating their flight and reducing water loss. Soaring and gliding migrants on the other hand migrate only during the day, landing to roost for the night. They circumvent water bodies, using longer migration routes that are usually well defined and regular, where soaring conditions and winds facilitate their flight. Since passive flight conserves energy, they do not have to store fat at the high levels active flyers do. Still and all, soaring flight is dependent on thermal creation, which prevents migration when weather conditions do not allow thermals to develop.

The picture on the screen of the approach radar at Ben-Gurion International Airport shows a large mass of passerines entering Israel across the Mediterranean coastline (the light line crossing the center of the picture from top to bottom), over the greater Tel-Aviv area, at an azimuth of 130 degrees (upper photo). At dawn the radar screen shows passerine migration in a north-south direction parallel to the coastline (lower photo).

D. How Birds Find Their Way on Migration

One of the most important and fascinating questions about migration is how birds navigate and find their way. Despite long years of research by many scientists, only part of this mystery has been solved. It is amazing how a tiny passerine, weighing only 10 grams, whose brain weighs only one-half a gram, departs on a migratory journey that can extend thousands of kilometers, without losing its way. All this, while repeating the same journey accurately, year after year, returning to the exact same spot to spend the winter (in autumn) and to breed (in spring). In order to find answers to this question scientists have studied a number of subjects: how do birds use information for navigating? Are they able to correct their route according to changing factors along the way, and what exactly are the limitations of their navigational abilities?

Navigation and visual memory   Navigation is especially complex and critical when we take into account the fact that in many bird species adults depart from their breeding quarters on migration, leaving their young behind. These young birds that up to this point knew only the immediate vicinity of the nest from which they fledged, leave several weeks later on their first migratory journey. They must navigate distances extending thousands of kilometers without having learnt anything from their parents about the route to their winter quarters.

One of the theories on how birds find their way is related to their outstanding visual acuity and to their ability to identify and remember details and landmarks. A bird flying at an altitude of 1000 meters above the ground has a range of vision of 150 kilometers (in optimal conditions, with no haze, fog or similar interference). A bird flying on a moonlit night, 2000 meters above the ground, can for example, discern lakes or other water bodies at a distance of 50-100 kilometers. In this manner birds use conspicuous topographical objects and other landmarks for navigating, and direct their flight to distant areas with suitable habitats. Ducks, for one, can point themselves directly to the next water body they see from a long distance. Woodland birds can fly directly to a wood or forest in their way, and so forth. Birds can choose a fixed migration direction and sustain it until they reach their wintering areas. This method however, is suitable only for short distances, and will not do for long-distance migration. In the latter case, a mistake of several degrees in direction can cause a deflection of hundreds, or even thousands of kilometers in navigation.

The best solution is the use of navigational abilities that allow route corrections as part of a migration plan directed to a predetermined goal. Another, similar possibility, is that instead of correcting its direction to a previously "programmed" goal, the bird will use landmarks for navigating, such as a river, mountain range, coastline, etc. A more sophisticated way is to exploit a combination of several celestial bodies or landmarks, while finding the relative direction to all of them simultaneously.

If birds do indeed employ various landmarks, including the relation between celestial bodies at night (changes in the starry sky and in sun location) for navigation, they must be equipped with an accurate internal clock that enables them to link between a time scale and variations in the landmarks that help them navigate. Such a clock, the circadian clock, exists and it makes it possible for birds to receive information on the time dimension. Experiments have shown that birds have an internal clock that corrects itself according to environmental changes that repeat themselves every 23-25 hours. These are variations in the cycle of light and dark that are received by the brain not only from the eyes but also directly through the skull. Various studies have shown that the hypothalamus, the part of the brain that receives stimuli from sensory organs, plays an important role in the regulation of body temperature. The hypothalamus is 100 times more sensitive than the retina of the eye to variations in the day-night cycle. Experiments have proven that hormones from the pineal gland in the brain control the sensory mechanism for light and dark. These stimuli are not necessarily in the visible light spectrum, but can originate in other wavelengths as well. It has also been proven conclusively that artificial lengthening of daylight and shortening of night (as in spring), induces significant gonad development, up to 80 times the normal size during a period of 20 days, and increased sperm production in males of various bird species. Increasing only the intensity of light on the other hand, (without changing the length of the light period and dark periods), does not produce similar results.

As mentioned above the internal biological clock of birds is invaluable for navigating with the help of celestial bodies and landmarks. Since the earth turns on its axis on a 24-hour cycle, each hour represents a 15-degree change in longitude, equivalent to 1800 kilometers along the Equator! A one-minute discrepancy in time evaluation can cause an error of 30 kilometers in distance! Thus, birds equipped with a precise mechanism for estimating time and its variations can exploit various ways for navigating and finding their way. Research has shown that birds use identification of salient landmarks and navigate by visual memory. Experiments on pigeons showed that they home directly on familiar objects, especially buildings close to the pigeon loft. Sea birds nesting on islands probably recognize the unique shape of "their" island, and home in on it the minute they see it. In this same manner birds apparently recognize landmarks in the area of their territory that helps them in the final stages of goal orientation, such as returning from migration to the exact same nest site year after year. Some birds were found to winter in the exact same site several years in a row. Among them are Wagtails that return year after year to the same yard, Chaffinches to the same garden or Kestrels to the same field. These birds too, apparently use visual memory in the final stages of arrival at winter quarters. This allows them to home exactly on the same spot each year. Some scientists claim that visual memory develops during a bird's life, and that each individual accumulates "pictures" of sites and landmarks it has seen in its memory. This claim has not yet been proven conclusively, but circumstantial evidence indicates that it may be valid. Adult birds that have migrated in the past leave on their journey rapidly and with confidence, while young that have not migrated before, in whose memory no "pictures" of the route and wintering sites have accumulated, leave hesitantly, first flying a short distance in order to gradually examine and learn the route.

Navigation using celestial bodies   Research done on various birds has shown that they are able to navigate by using the sun's position and relative height. Pigeons were found to determine the direction and height of the sun, not by looking

The Marsh Harrier migrates mainly by soaring and gliding, but since it has a low wing loading value it can also fly actively.
(Photo: Noah Satat)

Pages 72-73:
Black Kites gather to roost at sunset.
(Photo: Yossi Eshbol - The Society for the Protection of Nature in Israel Collection)

Page 75:
The Swift migrates by either active or
gliding flight for long distances.
(Photo: Eric and David Hosking FLPA)

at it directly, but at the shadow cast by various objects in their vicinity. This not only protects their eyes, but also as calculated from many experiments, allows them to determine the direction and height of the sun six times more accurately from shadows than by gazing directly at the sun. By using their sun compass birds can determine direction with an accuracy of 3 to 5 degrees, while altitude is determined much less accurately - by about 8 to11 degrees. Despite these limitations, if we take into account that a bird corrects its route while migrating by looking at the sun, and also uses landmarks, the sun compass is extremely useful in navigation.

Another factor that makes the sun important in navigation is the fact that it rises in the east and sets in the west. Experiments have shown that birds migrating at night use the setting sun to orientate in relation to their migration direction. This same principal probably works for the rising sun in birds that migrate during the day. Radar monitoring of migration has shown conclusively that many birds fly off shortly after sunset (nocturnal migrants), or sunrise (diurnal migrants). This fact too, confirms the importance of the direction of sunset and sunrise in bird orientation.

Although the moon is one of the most prominent celestial bodies, it is unlikely that birds rely on its relative position for navigating because of its complex movement in relation to the earth. The same principle applies to other planets. The stars, however, play a major role in the navigation of birds migrating at night. This has been proven in many laboratory experiments, some of which were done more than 50 years ago. In these experiments birds were placed in funnel-shaped cages whose bottoms were covered with ink and their sides with paper. Birds showed restlessness during migration and tried to fly off in the direction they were supposed to migrate in. The largest number of ink marks were "drawn" in the main direction they tried to fly and by this method their preferred direction could be determined. In most of these experiments birds were examined under natural starry skies and under planetarium skies which could be rotated artificially. When the planetarium sky was rotated, the birds changed direction accordingly. Other experiments have shown that some species do not rely on an inner clock in their star compass, and when the planetarium sky was rotated, their ability to orientate was unaffected. So it would seem that migrating birds (or some of them, since not all species were examined) identify the pattern of the starry sky and orientate accordingly. Some species use the North Star and the constellations around it for navigating. When these were displaced in the planetarium the birds became confused and disoriented. In addition, other experiments on passerines showed that the ability to identify the starry sky map and use it for navigating is not hereditary but learned. Young raised in captivity without being exposed to the natural night sky could not find their way later on in the planetarium.

In planetarium experiments birds were placed in funnel-shaped cages whose bottoms were covered with ink and their sides with paper. When the birds tried to fly off, their legs left ink marks on the paper in the main direction they intended to migrate (upper drawing). When the planetarium sky was rotated their flight direction changed accordingly (lower drawings).
(Drawing: Tuvia Kurtz)

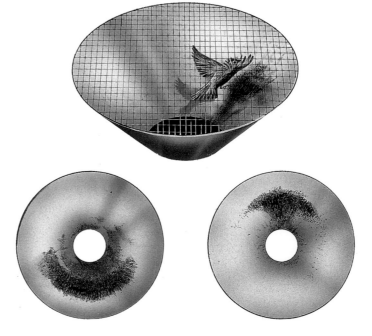

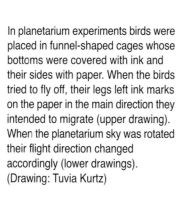

Cory's Shearwater migrates towards the Gulf of Eilat. It has a salt gland at the base of its bill for excreting excess salt that allows it to drink seawater.
(Photo: Hadoram Shirihai)

Magnetic fields   Another means birds have for navigating and orientating is the earth's magnetic field. In pigeons, a tiny organ located between the anterior part of the brain and the skull has approximately one hundred million needle-like particles, each 0.1 micron in length. These microscopic particles contain Magnetite that is extremely sensitive to changes in the magnetic field. In other birds similar organs have been found in the neck muscles, adjacent to the olfactory nerves in the head, and in the air channels connecting the nostrils and the pharynx. Experiments have shown that at least some birds are unable to identify the polar magnetic fields, and thus do not avail themselves of their ability to sense magnetic fields as a compass in north-south orientation. This is logical, since during the millions of years birds have inhabited the earth, the magnetic north has reversed itself many times. Instead, birds can avail themselves of their ability to sense the earth's magnetic field in order to find their direction and position in relation to latitude, by sensing changes in the magnitude of the magnetic field and its angle in relation to the earth's surface. The ability to sense changes in the magnetic field is probably a major tool in bird navigation, in addition to the other compasses described earlier. An expression of this importance has been found in studies from areas with abnormal magnetic fields, as a result of human disturbance (such as high-power transmitters, underwater communication systems and others), or natural geological phenomena in specific sites. In these cases birds have been found to depart from their usual migratory routes and display unusual flight behavior involving doubling the speed of wing movements and large energy losses.

Sound waves, taste and smell   Another common means by which birds navigate and orientate is the use of sound waves. In this case we refer not to the calls produced by birds migrating in a flock that are used for vocal communication in order to stay in touch, but to very low frequency sound waves outside the hearing range that are sensed by the inner ear. The human ear can hear frequencies as low as 10 Hertz. Experiments done on pigeons have shown that they react to frequencies as low as 0.06 Hertz, the type of frequency produced by sources such as waves breaking on the beach or strong winds hitting mountains. These sound waves spread over great distances and birds can hear them as far away as several hundred kilometers. In this manner a pigeon flying over land can receive information on the distance between it and the coast, or a large mountain range cutting across the continents.

Migrating White Storks stop to rest and "refuel" at a fishpond.
(Photo: Yig'al Livneh)

In addition to the navigational methods described so far, research has shown that birds use other methods to for orienting themselves, especially over short distances. Birds apparently use their sense of taste and smell (which are not well developed) to identify tastes and smell characteristic of a specific site, or of sites along their migration route. This is mostly true of sea birds, whose sense of smell is relatively developed compared to terrestrial species. They are apparently able to identify the chemical composition typical of sites along their migration route when drinking seawater (they excrete excess salt from a special gland at the base of their bills). Use of smell for orientation has also been found in pigeons, although less developed than in sea birds.

In short, according to studies done so far, birds possess the ability to navigate and orientate by a variety of methods. The sun compass, star compass and magnetic compass are probably the major tools of bird navigation. Nevertheless, each bird combines various navigation means according to its structure and adaptation to each one and according to environmental conditions. Research on this subject has so far uncovered only a small fraction of the amazing navigational ability of birds, and the future probably holds new discoveries.

E. Timing of Migration, Fat Storage and "Refueling"

Many times migrating birds fly over extensive areas of barren deserts, snowy mountains or large water bodies such as oceans, where food is unavailable to them. They are sometimes exposed to extreme weather conditions, such as below freezing temperatures, strong winds, rain, snow and other factors. In order to maximize the chances of completing their journey successfully the birds must time their migratory journey ideally, and equip themselves with energy reserves before leaving on their way, or while on it.

Changes in day length are the principal factor affecting migration timing. Nevertheless, birds are sensitive to a number of triggers that finally determine when they set off on their journey. Among these is weather, for example. Rainy, stormy weather can trigger early migration in autumn. On the other hand, some species that usually migrate south when autumn arrives will overwinter in their breeding quarters when winter weather is mild and allows them to find food. A good example of such behavior can be found in Israel: the Short-toed Eagle is a raptor that feeds mainly on snakes and other reptiles, and so is usually found in Israel only during the warm season, from spring to autumn, flying off to winter in Africa. In certain years, when the winter is relatively warm and dry, a small number of Short-toed Eagles deviate from their normal timing and overwinter in Israel.

Another factor directly affecting the timing of migration is food availability and man sometimes significantly affects this factor. The Red Kite, for example, an omnivorous bird of prey, once spent summers in southern Scandinavia, while now there are individuals found there during the whole year. This is explained by the relative abundance of available food, mainly garbage in dumps and meat remains thrown out near slaughterhouses, which enable the kites to winter in this northern area. The timing of migration is also dependent on the latitude at which the bird breeds. Populations of certain species, that breed in southern areas, usually start nesting before more northerly populations, due to the favorable weather conditions. As a result, in many cases, "southern" birds complete their breeding cycle earlier, and can migrate earlier. One such case is the Swift: populations breeding in Italy complete their breeding cycle at the end of July. The northern German Swift populations complete their nesting cycle at the beginning of August, while populations nesting in central Finland finish nesting only in the end of August or the beginning of September.

A Short-toed Eagle lowers its legs while hunting for snakes.
(Photo: Ofer Bahat)

Another factor significantly affecting the timing of migration is the distance the migrant must cover and the time it takes it to complete migration. This is especially true of long-distance migrants that spend considerable time on their migratory journey and must complete their breeding cycle rapidly before leaving on their way. The Arctic Warbler is one such case: it breeds in Scandinavia and Siberia, and winters in Southeast Asia. The population breeding in Norway arrives there from winter quarters in the Malay Archipelago, between 18 and 25 June, after having flown about 12,500 kilometers, and immediately start nesting. The young fledge in the beginning of August and a short while later already migrate south with their parents to their winter quarters. One of the conspicuous signs that migration is near in many birds is intensive feeding, with the objective of storing fat as "fuel" for their migratory journey. Research has shown that birds can gain up to 50% their normal weight by accumulating fat before migration. The fat is stored under the skin in various parts of the body, such as the sides of the abdomen and in the thoracic area. On migration stopovers the birds consume any available food to make up for fat lost on the way. Weak birds that have used up most of their fat reserves have been found to stopover longer in order to "refuel" and accumulate fat for the rest of their voyage.

Research on passerines has shown that the amount of fat stored by the bird is related to the distance it must cover in migration - the longer a species migrates the more fat it accumulates. Birds of four different European Sylvia warbler species were weighed in Morocco, before crossing the Sahara, while others were weighed in Nigeria, after the crossing. The weight difference between the birds before crossing the Sahara and those that had already crossed it was between 34-44%! In other words, flying over this extreme desert area, where almost no food is available, cost them a large percentage of their body weight because they had to "burn" such a large amount of energy. Waders and other waterfowl use considerable amounts of fat when they cross-seas without stopping. A Turnstone (a wader species) ringed in Alaska migrated south to Hawaii, 4,000 kilometers away, within only 4 days! During this non-stop migration it lost 20% of its body weight by using most of the fat it had stored in preparation for migration.

A migrating Black Kite feeding on carrion in the Negev.
(Photo: Paul Doherty)

The larger the bird, the more fat it can store and "carry". The amount of fat stored has a direct effect on the migratory range of a bird. In a study done on hummingbirds in North America whose weight is a mere 4.5 grams, it was found that 2 grams were composed of fat. This allows the hummingbird to migrate continuously for 26 hours, burning fat at a rate of 0.69 calories an hour. Its average flight speed is 40 kilometers per hour, so the hummingbird can fly 1,000 kilometers continuously using only its fat reserves, to reach its winter quarters in the Gulf of Mexico. Large avian species, such as geese, can fly actively for 6,000 kilometers by availing themselves of their fat reserves. Soaring birds, such as storks and large raptors, fly thousands of kilometers while migrating without having to "refuel", thanks to their energy-efficient flying method and their ability to store large amounts of fat.

The choice of migration route and the exploitation of food sources along it are very important in order for birds to conserve their fat reserves and renew them. Some birds tend to stopover on migration at sites where there is an abundance of food in order to rest and "refuel". The fields north of the city of Eilat in Israel are an example of these. Passerines and other birds migrating north in spring, fly over North Africa and Sinai, arid areas with scarce food and water. Eilat is the first site with a concentration of food, water and vegetation for some species after they have flown over extensive desert areas. Large numbers of birds stopover, some for a very short time, others for several days and even weeks. In the fields north of the city the birds find abundant and varied food and make good use of these conditions for rest, drinking and feeding before continuing on their journey.

The stork and the serpent

At the end of April 1984, at 20:30, Ofer Bahat was on his way to Jerusalem. In the Elah Valley, about one kilometer west of Kibbutz Netiv Ha-Lamed-heh, his headlights fell on a White Stork standing at the side of the road with what looked like a "rope" around its neck. He lowered his lights so as not to blind and frighten the stork, and proceeded slowly towards it. To his surprise he found that the "rope" that had seemed to be around its neck was a Black Coluber Snake the stork was in the midst of swallowing!! Its dark, uniform color showed it to be an adult snake, since the immature of this species are striped on a gray background. Only when they reach a length of about 1.4 meters do they take on a uniform, black color. The length of an adult Black Coluber Snake can reach 2.4 meters.

The size and length of the snake made it difficult for the stork to swallow it, which was why it was breathing heavily and not moving. The anterior part of the snake was deep in the stork's throat, but more than one meter of its body was hanging down and its tail dragged on the ground. After photographing this amazing sight Ofer Bahat waited nearby to see how events would develop. He was worried that cars passing in the area would hurt the stork that would have difficulty in moving away in its condition.

The stork continued standing in the same spot for 10 minutes and then suddenly spread its wings and with great effort flew heavily off to a nearby field, landing in the dark, apparently no more than about 15 meters from the road.

White Storks feed on a variety of foods - insects, fish, amphibians, chicks, rodents and various reptiles, including snakes (usually small ones). It is very difficult for a stork to swallow a snake as large as a Black Coluber Snake, but it would seem that the energy gained made the effort worthwhile!

Page 75:
The stork swallowing a black snake.
(Photo: Ofer Bahat)

Black Kites descending to rest, drink and hunt in the fields of Kibbutz Eilot, north of Eilat.
(Photo: Ofer Bahat)

Page 82:
Migrating Honey Buzzards over the Judean Desert cliffs.
(Drawing: James P. Smith)

Chapter 2

Israel -
A Crossroad between
Three Continents

נָתִיב לֹא יְדָעוֹ עָיִט וְלֹא שְׁזָפַתּוּ עֵין אַיָּה (איוב כ״ח, ז)

"That path no eagle knoweth,
Neither hath the Honey Buzzard's eye seen it."
(Job, 28:7)

A. *Israel's Unique Position on the World Migration Map*

Our ancestors were aware of the amazing phenomenon of mass migration of birds flying over Israel at regular times and routes as far back as biblical times: "That path no eagle knoweth, Neither hath the Honey Buzzard's eye seen it." (Job, 28 7). Israel is located at a geographical bridge between three continents - Europe, Asia and Africa, which makes it a "bottleneck" into which hundreds of migrant bird species converge during spring and autumn migration. Thanks to its unique location a vast variety of migrating species are found in Israel, despite its small size. The only comparable site in the world is Panama, the link between North and South America, where a great variety of migrating bird species also fly over in massive numbers.

As a result of this singular geographic location, the boundaries of many birds' distribution range occur in Israel. One such case is the Lappet-faced Vulture found in Africa and the Arabian Peninsula, or the Sooty Falcon, whose northern limit is in Israel. The range of the Striated Scops Owl, a small owl feeding mainly on insects, found in western China and southern Asia, reaches its western limit in Israel. The Blackbird, Great Tit, Wren, Tawny Owl and other species found in Europe and Asia, have their southern limit in Israel. As a result, a total of 530 different species can be seen in Israel. The number of species per area unit is also very high compared to other areas in the world as can be seen from the following data:

A Steppe Buzzard migrating over the Eilat Mountains.
(Photo: Paul Doherty)

Country	Area (km)	Number of species	Number of species per 1000 km
Israel	29,600	530	17.90
England	244,400	489	2.00
Germany	356,500	258	0.73
Egypt	990,000	427	0.43
Sudan	2,500,000	371	0.35
China	9,800,000	1,198	0.12
USSR (formerly)	22,400,000	728	0.03

Soaring birds circumvent large water bodies such as the Mediterranean, Caspian, Black, Red Sea and others, so they choose crossing points where the distance across water is minimal. As a result, the western European soaring bird population converges over the Strait of Gibraltar when migrating to Africa. A small portion of the central European population crosses the Mediterranean at its narrowest sections, such as the point between Sicily and North Africa. The major part of the northern, central and eastern European populations, as well as soaring birds from Asia and the Caucasus, migrate along the shortest route that circumvents the Mediterranean to the east, and converge in the skies of Israel on their way to Africa in autumn and back in spring.

Because of their great weight soaring birds are unable to use flapping flight continuously, except for short periods of time. They must therefore use migration routes over areas where soaring conditions are optimal. Soaring bird migration thus

Page 84:
The Lappet-faced Vulture in this photo is one of the two last individuals that bred in Israel, nesting in the southern Arava Valley (1987).
(Photo: Hadoram Shirihai)

converges into long and narrow valley, cliffs and mountainous areas, where soaring conditions are best.

Soaring birds glide from thermal to thermal, locating the next thermal along the way by sight (they see other birds soaring on the next thermal) or with the help of the extreme sensitivity of their wings and bodies to any change in air currents.

Israel's principal advantage as a migration route for soaring birds is based primarily on it geomorphologic location. The Syrian-African Rift cuts the country from the Hula Valley in the north, down along the Jordan Valley, the Dead Sea and the Arava, to the Gulf of Eilat in the south, and is an ideal area for thermal formation. The width of the rift in this area is not great, but the difference in altitude between the deep center to the high sides can reach hundred of meters (such as along the Fault Escarpment in the Judean Desert), causing adiabatic warming of the air. The combination of steep cliffs, cut by narrow gorges and high average temperatures along the rift during migration seasons, create excellent flight conditions for soaring birds.

The line of mountain ranges that starts in the Lebanese mountains in the north, on south along the Galilee mountains and the Samarian and Judean mountains, lies almost parallel to the coastline. Winds (including the sea breeze) that hit the mountains are displaced upwards, creating excellent gliding conditions, which greatly facilitate soaring bird migration. Soaring bird migration tracking over the past three decades, between Europe and Asia to Africa, and between North and South America, has proven that these birds converge on straits and along geomorphologic lines where soaring conditions are optimal, avoiding large water bodies.

As a result, crossing points at the various straits along the migration route (such as Gibraltar, Bosporus, Dardanelles, the Gulf of Eilat and Bab el Mandeb) function

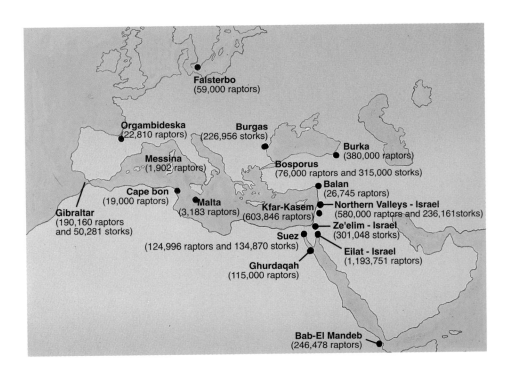

Stork and raptor survey stations in the Mediterranean Basin.
(Drawing: Tuvia Kurtz)

as "bottlenecks" into which most soaring birds converge. These well defined "bottlenecks" have been of great help to migration research, allowing various subjects to be studied, such as the time it takes different species to cross, the number of individuals crossing and how they vary over the years.

The magnitude of soaring bird migration is variable. Of 285 known diurnal raptor species at least 133 (about 47%) migrate with some sort of frequency. Partial migration is the most common (91 species). Twenty-four species migrate partially or wander and only 18 migrate totally. Total migration is defined as the passage of the entire population of a given species from continent to continent. In partial migration part of the population remains in its continent of origin. Wandering is a situation in which populations stay on the same continent moving only locally.

In the past little was known about soaring bird migration outside the boundaries of Europe and North America. During the last two decades significant progress has been made in the study of raptor migration in Israel. The earliest observations were made by Uriel Safriel and published in 1968. As a result, a group of Danish birdwatchers headed by Steen Christiensen counted the migrating raptors over the Eilat area between 1969 and 1978. In spring 1977 they counted 763,737 birds of prey above the Eilat mountains. From this they estimated that millions of raptors fly over Israel annually during spring migration.

At the same time migration was being studied in Eilat, Ehud Dovrat discovered a major raptor migration route in autumn 1977. This route passes over the fields of Kfar Qasem and along the western slopes of the Samarian and Judean mountains. Detailed surveys organized by the Society for the Protection of Nature in Israel's Raptor Information Center, showed that hundreds of thousands of birds of prey fly along this route every autumn. The data gathered from the autumn raptor migration surveys at Kfar Qasem launched a new series of studies. In Eilat, Hadoram Shirihai coordinated a series of raptor migration surveys under the auspices of the Israel Raptor Information Center, and eventually as part of the research in the International Birdwatching Center at Eilat. These surveys enlarged on the work done by the Danish birdwatchers in the past. In spring 1985, 1,193,751 birds of prey were counted over the Eilat mountains, the highest number ever counted in Israel during one migratory season. This number is far beyond that found at almost any other migration sites in the world. The only two exceptions are raptor migration over Panama, between North and South America, where similar numbers were counted and Costa Rica. During autumn migration, three times more birds of prey than in Eilat were counted in Costa Rica.

Local surveys were done at different locations in Israel, such as Bet Shemesh, Afula, Beersheba and Rosh Pinna, supplying vast, interesting information on raptor migration over Israel. These surveys showed that sometimes extremely high numbers of raptors concentrated in one or two days pass over Israel! One such case was recorded at Kfar Qasem on 10-11 September 1982, when 241,676 Honey Buzzards were counted. This is equivalent to 75.6% of the total number of Honey Buzzards counted during the entire migration season!

The vast number of birds converging from millions of square kilometers to pass over Israel within only a few days, raised the question of what factor is responsible for concentrating them in passage with such accurate timing. Israel's unique location on the global migration map, and the preliminary data gathered made it imperative to organize a broad, in-depth study and to develop methods to find solutions to the many unanswered questions. Is there any annual and seasonal (spring and autumn) regularity in the number of migrating birds, their times of arrival and the length of their migration waves? Is there regularity in the horizontal and vertical migration routes over Israel and their velocity, on a daily, seasonal and annual scale How do climatic and biological factors affect the migration season, and is it possible to predict variations in migration characteristics according to them. These questions will be answered in the following sections.

A light-phase Booted Eagle migrating in the Eilat area.
(Photo: Ofer Bahat)

B. Soaring birds migrating over Israel

Migration surveys in Israel have shown that 35 different species of diurnal birds of prey fly over Israel during autumn and spring migration. Other species of soaring birds such as White Storks, Black Storks, White Pelicans, Dalmatian Pelicans and Cranes, pass over as well. Hundreds of thousands of Honey Buzzards, Steppe Buzzards and White Storks fly over Israel and are the commonest soaring migrants. A bit less prevalent are tens of thousands of migrating Levant Sparrowhawks, Lesser Spotted Eagles, Steppe Eagles, Black Kites and White Pelicans. The Short-toed Eagle, Booted Eagle, Marsh Harrier and Red-footed Falcon are less common, and between 1000 to 10,000 fly over each migration season.

Pages 88-89:
Honey Buzzards do not usually feed during migration, but sometimes stop to drink. The Honey Buzzard in the photograph stopped to drink at a puddle in the Eilat area.
(Photo: Yossi Eshbol)

Lesser Kestrels, Sparrowhawks, Egyptian Vultures and other harrier species are relatively rare, and up to 1000 individuals of each species have been counted. The rarest species, with up to 100 of each counted, are the Osprey, Imperial Eagle, Spotted Eagle, Pallid Harrier and Dalmatian Pelican.

Some species probably fly over in greater numbers than noted above. However, due to the difficulty of counting all individuals, mainly because of the great altitude they fly at or the fact that some fly over areas not covered by the observation stations, these are only estimates at this stage. Nevertheless, and in order to illustrate the number of birds flying over Israel during the migration seasons, several examples of totals counted in migration surveys by ground-based observers are brought below (the data relates to the most prevalent migrant soaring birds species, of which 1000 or more individuals were counted during at least some of the survey years):

The total number of major soaring bird species counted in autumn migration surveys between 1982-1990

Species	Kfar Qasem - Cross-Samaria Survey						Northern Valleys Survey		
	1982	1983	1984	1985	1986	1987	1988	1989	1990
Short-toed Eagle	7142	7697	7399	7005	8045	7288	3008	2492	3819
Lesser Spotted Eagle	89239	141868	88210	108873	114446	81429	74198	56533	83701
Booted Eagle	1176	1267	1127	1498	1973	1304	622	842	811
Steppe Buzzard	80	303	139	352	517	461	934	2166	1952
Honey Buzzard	319660	133621	380576	390612	419164	379672	347397	300972	437432
Black Kite	313	293	447	759	1051	1195	1063	1131	1734
Marsh Harrier	398	476	587	801	1237	1236	751	1534	1516
Levant Sparrowhawk	21983	25316	29255	37896	44653	28708	40560	41237	41722
Sparrowhawk	385	513	813	592	1761	1317	620	1150	868
Red-footed Falcon	631	1097	1514	2820	5752	1833	2836	4942	4200
Total no. Raptors	445317	316459	514622	556756	603846	508676	474458	417073	580617
White Stork						202935	176322	146904	236161
White Pelican						65569	76909	76523	68539

The total number of major raptor species counted in spring migration surveys in Eilat and storks counted in the western Negev

Species	1977	1983	1985	1986	1987	1988	1989	1990
Steppe Eagle	19288	23318	75073	22762	17443	10922		
Steppe Buzzard	315767	109493	225460	465827	380441	429139		
Black Kite	26770	27039	28834	24728	31363	31774		
Levant Sparrowhawk	5958	2556	905	17034	49836	21380		
Honey Buzzard	225952	265775	851598	341777	293658	188914		
Total no. raptors	763737	474127	1193751	873388	778224	688659		
Total no. storks					294754	301048	248822	219191

This Buzzard hunted in Kleia, southern Lebanon, is exhibited on a car bumper. (Photo: Rafi Kopen)

C. Migrating Birds - Chances of Survival

Migrating birds pass through many different countries on their journey and are exposed to numerous threats and dangers. Entire populations of bird species migrate from Europe and Asia to Africa over a narrow land strip, (mainly in the Middle East and Sinai), which constitutes a "bottleneck" into which millions of birds converge. For this reason it is of major importance to protect birds along their migration route and to prevent harm coming to them, since this could endanger entire bird populations, some of rare, endangered species.

Tribes in southern Sudan hunt migrating White Storks for food while they feed in rivers.
(Photo: Pierre Perrin)

Stork trapping by Sudanese hunters.
(Photo: Pierre Perrin)

A Sudanese hunter carrying a dead White Stork.
(Photo: Pierre Perrin)

Sudanese children plucking the hunted stork before cooking it.
(Photo: Pierre Perrin)

Hunting   When examining the dangers migrating birds are exposed to in contrast to their chances of survival the picture is quite dismal at times. There is a long tradition of hunting in Mediterranean countries and the number of hunters is sometimes hundreds of times greater than the number of nature lovers and conservationists. Israel is an exception to this rule in the area. All birds of prey and most other species as well, are protected by law from harm of any sort (except for certain extremely common species, or agricultural pests, such as the House Sparrow, Chukar and a few others). The number of active bird-watchers and nature lovers in Israel is also significantly greater in relation to the total population than in other Mediterranean countries. This situation is a result of intensive educational activity by the Society for the Protection of Nature in Israel since it was established in 1954 and by the Israel Nature Reserves Authority established in 1963. Consequently, only rarely is a migrating bird shot by hunters in the country.

In other Mediterranean and Middle Eastern countries, on the other hand, there is massive destruction of migrating birds from unrestricted hunting. The table below (based on Report on Bird Killing in the Mediterranean, by S. Woldhek, 1980), presents data on the number of hunters compared to the number of bird lovers in various countries in the Mediterranean Basin, painting a gloomy picture of the situation in the area (there is no data for countries not appearing in the table):

Country	Number of Hunters	Number of Bird Lovers (estimate)	Proportion of Bird Lovers / Hunters
Lebanon	400,000	10	1:40,000
Turkey	3,000,000	100	1:30,000
Morocco	30,000	10	1:3,000
Italy	2,230,000	1,000	1:2,230
Cyprus	30,000	20	1:1,500
Greece	242,000	200	1:1,210
Yugoslavia (formerly)	220,000	200	1:1,100
France	2,100,000	2,000	1:1,050
Portugal	200,000	200	1:1,000
Spain	1,000,000	2,000	1:500
Tunisia	8,000	20	1:400
Jordan	5,000	20	1:250
Malta	15,500	550	1:23
Israel	5,000	4,000	1:1.25

A hunter in Rashaya, Lebanon, slings dead warblers he shot on his belt, before preparing dinner from them. (Photo: Yossi Leshem)

The data in the table above illustrate the grim hunting situation in Mediterranean countries. Even more serious is the fact that in some countries, such as France, where most migrating birds, for instance raptors, are protected by law, it is almost impossible to enforce hunting regulations, apprehend and try hunters that have broken the law. It is not hard to imagine the damage caused by millions of hunters roaming open spaces and shooting at anything that moves.

Lebanon is the Middle Eastern country in which raptor slaughter reaches its peak. Anyone used to seeing and hearing birds is in for a sad surprise when traveling around Lebanon: there are almost no birds to be seen. Armed villagers roam the country and during migration seasons hunting becomes the "national sport". Shotguns and other weapons can be found in every household and cartridge shells abound - a silent testimony to the continuous, destructive hunting. Stuffed animals, mainly of raptors and colorful songbirds such as Orioles and Bee-eaters among others, are a common sight in many store windows. Caged songbirds for sale are found in many yards and raptors or storks that were hunted for "sport" or target practice are proudly displayed. In Lebanon, as in most Mediterranean countries, the majority of birds are protected by law. This protection, however is *de jure* only and not observed by anyone. International conservation organizations have found that 15 to 20 million birds are hunted in Lebanon annually. Lebanese visiting Syria hunt an additional 5 to 10 million birds. It should be noted that these numbers are based on past estimates and the current situation is probably much worse.

A store selling washers in the Damascus market has a sideline of stuffed raptors hunted in Syria during migration (upper photo). Stuffed birds of prey and foxes are sold as souvenirs at the duty-free shop at Damascus Airport. On the left is a photo of Syria's president, Hafez Assad (lower photo).

An Egyptian hunter at Suez holding two Steppe Eagles he shot for sport.
The eagles in the photo are still alive and holding their heads up.
(Photo: David Wimphiemer)

One method of passerine hunting is glue-covered bush branches that the bird sticks to when perching with no possibility of escape. Songbirds are eaten, a practice prevalent in all Mediterranean countries, where canned bird-meat is a common delicacy. In Syria too, massive carnage of migrating birds, mainly birds of prey, is common. This wholesale killing is so much a part of life that stuffed eagles, buzzards and many other raptors can be found on sale in the duty-free shop at Damascus International Airport. In addition to stuffed birds, live birds of prey that were trapped, such as vultures and eagles, are held chained in appalling conditions, and displayed for potential buyers in the Damascus market.

Birds of prey are exposed to hunting at many other sites along their migration route not only in the Mediterranean area. There is data on massive hunting of migrating birds crossing the Caucasian Mountains in the Georgian Republic, for instance. Birds are also exposed to hunting in their winter quarters in Africa, where they are hunted for food in countries where famine is widespread, such as Sudan, with bows and arrows, spears or even by hand.

This marked Egyptian Vulture, photographed at the Sede Boqer raptor feeding station in summer 1987 about three weeks after fledging, has a transmitter on its back, a wing-tag and rings on its legs.
(Photo: Yossi Eshbol)

The marked Egyptian Vulture in adult plumage, at the Khartoum Zoo in January 1993.
(Photo: Dr. Ernst Dieter)

The "Israeli spy" arrived in Sudan

"In October 1989 the first Israeli spy ever was caught at the border of Sudan and Chad in Africa, 4,000 kilometers from Israel". This report appeared in the African military publication African Defense, in the December 1989 issue. The spy was described as a "large, dark falcon originating in Palestine". After a copy of the article arrived in Israel, it became clear that this was one of the young Egyptian Vultures Nadav Levi had attached transmitters to, as part of his graduate work on the ecology and biology of this species in Israel.

Three years later, Professor Heinrich Mendelssohn of the Tel-Aviv University Zoology Department received a letter from Dr. Ernst Dieter, a German scientist from Hamburg, lecturing in Zoology at Khartoum University, who managed to find out that the "spying" Egyptian Vulture was being held at the Khartoum Zoo, after having been caught in the Dafur area, near El Gateina in western Sudan. The photograph he sent finally verified that this was one of the three adult Egyptian Vultures that had been trapped, ringed, marked with wing tags and had transmitters attached, as part of Nadav Levi's research. The vulture had been marked and immediately released in late July 1987. During the next two years it was seen again twice not far from where it was originally caught in the summer of 1988.

A similar story was published in many other newspapers in the Middle East and Europe in September 1977: A pelican with a transmitter attached was seen in Sudan and the Sudanese government claimed the Mossad (Israeli intelligence) was spying on them. On 22 September 1997 the following article appeared in Ma'ariv, one of Israel's daily newspapers:

"Sudan is planning to lodge a complaint against Israel for using pelicans for spying. The sources reported to the weekly that Sudan noticed Israel was using pelicans that fly from it to other countries in the region and attaching various spying instruments to them, and that the transmitters attached to the pelicans weigh about 100 grams. Sources added that the Israeli Mossad is responsible for these actions."

We believe this to be one of the White Storks with transmitters attached that are part of the joint project by the Max Planck Institute in Germany and Tel-Aviv University, as it was migrating over Sudan.

A flying stork on a "spit"

On 22 April 1988, at the peak of spring migration, Nadav Levi, an Israeli ornithologist, saw several dozen White Storks land to roost in Sede-Tsin in southern Israel, not far from Kibbutz Sede Boqer. He was amazed to see that one of the storks had an arrow about a meter long embedded in. The stork behaved naturally and fed with the rest of the flock before it gathered to roost. The arrow was probably shot by an African hunter, in one of the countries where European storks winter, such as Sudan, Kenya or Tanzania.

There is an extreme shortage of food in the countries located along the Syrian-African Rift so that the inhabitants of these areas sometimes hunt storks for food. The arrow apparently entered through the stork's wing, the wound healed, and the stork was forced to live on with an unwanted "appendage"...

The next morning Nadav Levi saw the stork again along with the late Major Gidi Zakai, a pilot and birdwatcher. The stork joined a flock of about 5,000 others and at about 10 A.M. they flew off on their way to Europe.

Nadav succeeded in photographing the stork with the arrow implanted in it. Another, similar photograph taken in Poland was later received in Israel, showing a White Stork with a spear through it that had made its way from Africa to Poland...

The White Stork with an arrow imbedded in it flying over Sede Tsin. (Photo: Nadav Levi)

The Saudi King's Falcon Fled to Sharm al Sheikh

In late March 1982, Dr. Dani Simon from Tel-Aviv University found a dead Saker Falcon that belonged to King Haled of Saudi Arabia, in the Sharm ash Sheikh area in southern Sinai. On its leg was a ring engraved with the inscription: "the king's son Haled ibn Abdul Aziz Abdallah ibn Haled ibn Abdul Aziz".

This falcon was one of at least a hundred trained falcons belonging to King Haled, used for hunting, mainly Houbara Bustards (a large desert bird). The falcon apparently fled its trainers, crossed the Arabian Peninsula and the Red Sea, finally arriving in southern Sinai, probably completely exhausted.

The Saker Falcon is one of the largest falcons, and considered excellent for falconry (raptor training for hunting). Its wingspan is 1.25 meters and it can stoop to its prey at a speed of 300 kilometers per hour. The price of a trained Saker Falcon can reach tens of thousands of dollars. Use of Saker Falcons and other large falcons, such as the Peregrine, for falconry, has greatly harmed their natural populations.

Many falcons are trapped for this purpose in their breeding territories or while migrating over the Middle East, their young and eggs stolen from their nest, after which they are trained and sold. Some trained falcons, such as this one, escape their trainers, but in many cases are unable to adapt to their natural environment and cannot survive.

Stamps from Bahrain showing the use of trained falcons for hunting, a common practice in the Arabian Peninsula.

A dark-phase Booted Eagle that drifted over the sea and drowned while migrating was found on the Palmahim beach in Israel.
(Photo: Kobi Merom)

A White Pelican shot by fishermen in the Hula Valley and hung up near a fish pond as a warning to its friends.
(Photo: Guido Kiel)

Weather conditions   Another factor which can significantly affect the survival of migrating birds is weather. Sudden changes in weather and development of extreme conditions can be critical for many birds. One such case occurred in Israel during the second week in April 1980. A sudden change in weather brought on strong easterly winds and in their wake a precipitous fall in temperatures and rain. The strong easterly winds carried hundreds of birds of prey, storks and other birds west into the sea. Most of these birds were unable to fly back to the coast and drowned and many of their bodies were washed ashore. More than 1,100 buzzards, close to 150 eagles, 75 White Storks, 8 Griffon Vultures, 8 Egyptian Vultures and many other birds were found in a survey that covered most of the beaches in Israel.

Confrontations with farmers   Agriculture poses many problems for migrating birds. Besides the extensive use of pesticides there are direct conflicts with farmers over food, especially in areas where birds overwinter for several months. In Israel, one of the major examples is the case of birds feeding on fish such as pelicans and cormorants that descend on fishponds causing severe damage to the fishery industry. Another case is that of birds such as cranes that feed on agricultural crops like peanuts or chickpeas. The farmers use various methods to chase the migrating and wintering birds away and minimize the damage they suffer from them. In several cases protected wintering birds have been shot. This conflict can probably only be solved by scientific research of the various factors affecting migrant bird feeding and the possibility of concentrating them in areas where damage would be minimal.

The Lanner Falcon that migrated to Saudi Arabia

A male Lanner Falcon that hatched on 18 March 1990 at the Tel-Aviv University Zoo was ringed with ring number G-18719, and included in a breeding nucleus intended for release into the wild. This nucleus was formed for release in the Ramat Hanadiv area in the Carmel, as part of a rare raptor breeding project aimed at releasing birds in nature, headed by Ohad Hatzofe under the auspices of the Rothschild Foundation and the Society for the Protection of Nature in Israel. This Lanner hatched from an egg laid by a Lanner pair in the Tel-Aviv University Zoo, that was moved to an incubator seven days after it was laid.

The chick spent its first four days with other chicks and then was removed to a female Lanner that raised it with her own young. Twenty-eight days after it hatched the young Lanner was moved, with another four chicks (from three different clutches) to Ramat Hanadiv, for acclimation in a special cage set up on the western escarpment of the Carmel. On 1 May 1990 the cage was opened and the birds set free. The Lanner was seen flying well with the other young falcons in the Ramat Hanadiv area. Five weeks after its release it left the area along with its companions, although some of them were later seen again in the area as part of the wandering process.

The young Lanner that had been released in Israel roamed for great distances, not realizing that unlike the caring treatment it had received in Israel danger lay across the border. In October 1990, about 5 months after it was released in the southern Carmel, a Bedouin in the vicinity of Jedda in Saudi Arabia trapped the Lanner, about 1,600 kilometers south of its release site. Lanners are not considered appropriate for falconry (hunting with trained falcons) and the bird was apparently trapped for use as bait for trapping Peregrines and Saker Falcons.

Page 101:
A Lanner Falcon released from captivity feeding on a Quail it hunted.
(Photo: Eyal Bartov)

Six White Pelicans that drifted over the Mediterranean and drowned, washed ashore at Habonim beach in Israel.
(Photo: Yig'al Livneh)